Refiguring **ENGLISH STUDIES** Refiguring English Studies provides a forum for scholarship on English studies as a discipline, a profession, and a vocation. To that end, the series publishes historical work that considers the ways in which English studies has constructed itself and its objects of study; investigations of the relationships among its constituent parts as conceived in both disciplinary and institutional terms; and examinations of the role the discipline has played or should play in the larger society and public policy. In addition, the series seeks to feature studies that, by their form or focus, challenge our notions about how the written "work" of English can or should be done and to feature writings that represent the professional lives of the discipline's members in both traditional and nontraditional settings. The series also includes scholarship that considers the discipline's possible futures or that draws upon work in other disciplines to shed light on developments in English studies.

Volumes in the Series

Stephen Parks, *Class Politics: The Movement for the Students' Right to Their Own Language* (2000)

Charles M. Anderson and Marian M. MacCurdy, editors, *Writing and Healing: Toward an Informed Practice* (2000)

Anne J. Herrington and Marcia Curtis, *Persons in Process: Four Stories of Writing and Personal Development in College* (2000)

Amy Lee, *Composing Critical Pedagogies: Teaching Writing as Revision* (2000)

Derek Owens, *Composition and Sustainability: Teaching for a Threatened Generation* (2001)

Chris W. Gallagher, *Radical Departures: Composition and Progressive Pedagogy* (2002)

Robert P. Yagelski and Scott A. Leonard, editors, *The Relevance of English* (2002)

Professing and Pedagogy

Learning the Teaching of English

SHARI J. STENBERG
Creighton University

National Council of Teachers of English
1111 W. Kenyon Road, Urbana, Illinois 61801-1096

Excerpts from "Teacher Narratives as Interruptive: Toward Critical Colleagueship" by Chris W. Gallagher, Peter M. Gray, and Shari Stenberg reprinted from SYMPLOKĒ, volume 10, numbers 1–2, by permission of the University of Nebraska Press. Copyright © SYMPLOKĒ 2002.

Manuscript Editor: Lee Erwin
Staff Editor: Bonny Graham
Interior Design: Jenny Jensen Greenleaf
Cover Design: Barbara Yale-Read

NCTE Stock Number: 37415

ISSN 1073-9637

©2005 by the National Council of Teachers of Engli

Library of Congress Cataloging-in-Publication Data

Stenberg, Shari J.
    Professing and pedagogy : learning the teaching of English / Shari J. Stenberg.
        p. cm. — (Refiguring English studies)
    Includes bibliographical references and index.
    ISBN 0-8141-3741-5 (pbk.)
  1. English philology—Study and teaching. 2. English teachers—Training of. I. Title. II. Series.
    PE66 .S74 2005
    428' .0071'1—dc22

2004023725

3714664

For Zoe, who helps me see with new eyes

CONTENTS

ACKNOWLEDGMENTS

A good friend of mine recently said, "When you are a teacher yourself, finding your own teacher is a true gift." I am blessed with many teachers who have influenced this book both directly and indirectly.

Steve North's commitment to high ideals and innovative visions has taught me much about teaching and writing. His integrity has taught me much about life.

Amy Lee planted the seed for this book through her inspiring teaching. Our ongoing conversations have nurtured and sustained both the book and its writer.

Chris Gallagher has been the most generous and helpful of readers, responding to nearly as many drafts of this book as have been written (and that's *many*) with great care and insight.

My hope is that this book will be a testament to the teaching I've learned from Steve, Amy, and Chris, which serves as a guide and an inspiration to me daily.

Greg Zacharias is a mentor, colleague, and friend like no other. I am exceptionally grateful for his wisdom, compassion, and guidance, which he shares generously.

Katie Stahlnecker read a very early draft of this book and cheered me on with gusto. Her friendship and faith have bolstered me through the process.

Susan Aizenberg has taught me much about writing, teaching, and life. In all of these areas, she encourages me to take risks and be bold.

My students are an endless resource of energy and inspiration. I am especially grateful to Krista Stock, Katie Wudel, Sarah Stanley, Jason Arthur, and Darby Arant for their teaching, learning, and colleagueship. The composition teachers at Creighton have welcomed me with open arms, contributed more than they are required, and provided community that sustains me.

Acknowledgments

Though I don't know them personally, the writings of Jennifer Gore, Elizabeth Ellsworth, and the late Mimi Orner have not only dramatically influenced my ideas about teaching, but have created a space for me to contribute my own. My work would not exist without theirs.

I am grateful to the NCTE reviewers—particularly Joy Ritchie—for comments that sparked new ideas and directions. Kurt Austin has been a patient and helpful editor; I am thankful for his guidance.

Because Larry Gillick and Jim Larrabee live out their passions and commitments, they help me see my teaching and my life anew, and prompt me toward ongoing revision.

My parents, Richard and Diane Stenberg, teachers of thirty-five years, were my own first teachers, and showed by example that teaching and learning can be a way of life. They provided a foundation of love and support that enabled me to change and grow; this is the best gift teachers give.

The writing process is not only intellectually but also emotionally intensive.

My husband, Jason Keese, has been my partner through every step of this project. His patience, perspective, and love not only guide me, but also remind me of what matters most.

My daughter, Zoe, is my light. May she have teachers like those I have had, who inspire her to love learning, and never to cease.

This project was supported by a Creighton Faculty Research Fellowship, sponsored by the Creighton Graduate School.

INTRODUCTION

M andi, a graduate school–bound senior English major, is facilitating discussion in our composition theory class. The topic is teaching, now vitally important to her as she struggles to imagine herself as an instructor of record in the fall. She offers the following prompt for our writing: "Describe a teacher. Don't think too much, just jot down what first comes to mind."

I begin to scrawl in my notebook, deliberately trying not to censor or overthink my response. I picture Mrs. Carlson, my fourth-grade teacher. I jot down "maternal" and "disciplinarian." She (definitely a she) is someone who is caring and nurturing, but who makes sure the students remain "in line." Susan Miller's metaphor of nurse-mother pops into my head: the teacher is responsible for passing along accepted knowledge and behaviors, and yet she is not adequately valued in the culture that depends on the very knowledge she supplies (1991, 137).

This person is not a professor, I write, and underline it. I stop and think: I've now been working for nearly seven years on a project that aims to disrupt the teacher/professor binary. And yet the distinction remains deeply ingrained in my mind.

Mandi asks us to stop writing, and invites volunteers to share their responses. After a brief silence, Mandi shares her own. "I pictured someone male," she says. "He is very authoritative about the knowledge in his field. He wears a suit, maybe a bow tie." We chuckle; she is describing a professor in our department.

Kristie goes next. "Mine is different," she points out. "When you said 'who is a teacher,' I pictured my K–12 instructors. I don't consider my professors teachers. I don't refer to them as teachers. I call them professors." For Kristie, the teacher is a woman. She's creative, and she wears bright-colored sweaters. Glasses hang from a chain around her neck.

"Yes, and she always has nice handwriting," Nancy adds.

And she's good at the "teacher grip," Philip interjects. He's met with blank looks. Didn't any of you ever get the teacher grip when you were in trouble?" The rest of the class, all women, laugh and shake our heads.

Other students agree that professors are an altogether different species. They are masters of their subject matter. They stand at the front of the room, facing students lined in neat rows. They lecture. Their authority stems from their knowledge, not their potential to discipline. "It's funny that I picture this," Mandi contends, "because none of my professors is really like this. And certainly I'm not going to teach like this."

As we discuss the differences we've learned (if not experienced) between the teacher and the professor, Mandi realizes that she, too, has learned them as entirely different categories. "I think one reason I don't see my professors as teachers," she reasons, "is that they aren't trained as teachers. They're trained as scholars."

And now that she faces teaching at the college level, she wonders how she will learn to teach. She is especially anxious because her careful research of graduate programs has produced very little evidence of resources for teacher learning. In fact, she leans toward accepting the offer made by the institution that seems to provide the most support for new teachers.

After class, I think about how Mandi's interest in the teacher-development process puts her far ahead of where I was at that stage. Like Mandi, I applied for graduate school my senior year of college, and had no experience teaching. The committee who reviewed my application and awarded me with an assistantship had seen only my personal statement of intended study, three writing samples, transcripts, and letters of recommendation. My perceived potential as a scholar, it seemed, qualified me to teach. And since teaching is what I was certain I wanted to do, I was only too glad to accept this presumption.

It was my mom, a middle school teacher of thirty-five years, who questioned the logic of this system, asking, "How can they ask you to teach without providing any methods courses?" The only way I knew how to answer this was that a professor (or even a professor-to-be) was a scholar, something different from a

teacher. I had learned—without its ever being spoken explicitly—
that the preparation to be a professor was distinct from the training to be a teacher. I gave my mother the answer I thought to be
true: graduate school fosters one's enrichment as a scholar, an
intellectual, a professor, and the teaching part naturally falls into
place.

This exchange with my mother—which stayed with me long
after we hung up the phone—became an initial catalyst for this
book. My mother's question invited me to wonder along with
her: How do we learn to be professors of English? But it did
more than that; it also invited me to look with different eyes at
the deep division between teachers and scholars. In fact, my response to her made abundantly clear that I had not only learned
the professor's work to be privileged above that of the teacher's,
but that I understood the process of learning to profess—mastery of scholarship—to be sufficient preparation for teaching.
Teaching, as I saw it, was the by-product of scholarly knowledge, not a means of *making* knowledge.

While I soon discovered that my response represented the
normative assumptions about professing—and professorial preparation—in the field, I also learned that this model has not gone
unchallenged. I did not, in fact, have to look far to see revisionary work in progress: the doctoral program I attended, SUNY–
Albany's Teaching, Writing, and Criticism, certainly defied
traditional assumptions about professing.[1] Formerly a D.A. program, the curriculum sought to make pedagogy an activity deserving of inquiry, a praxis one studied in dialogue with composition, literature, creative writing, or theory. This is not a new
idea for those of us in composition, where questions of how we
teach cannot be severed from what we teach. But it departs significantly from the dominant tendency to split doctoral education into two categories: scholarly work (i.e., seminars, exams,
dissertation) and the work that supports it, teaching. As a teaching assistant, one teaches to "pay" for one's study. Thus, support
for teaching is usually inextricably linked to the first-year writing program, and sponsored by a single writing program administrator, who works under pressure to train new teachers as quickly
and efficiently as possible to teach within an already established
program.

Here, too, my experience was somewhat unusual. My first teaching experiences did not take place in a first-year writing classroom; we had no such program. Nor did we have the "teacher-training" program that usually accompanies it. Instead, I spent most of my graduate teaching as one of about eight TAs, adjuncts, and faculty members working within our new Writing Sequence, a concentration in rhetoric and poetics for English majors. While I go into detail about this experience in Chapter 4, I will sketch some of its characteristics here. We teachers—who ranged from full professors to adjuncts to graduate TAs—met on a biweekly basis not only to discuss pedagogical issues, but also to examine and rethink our shared curriculum. We found ways to include students in our discussion of the curriculum; they helped us understand the connections among our courses and to consider ways of fostering writing development over a sequence of courses. Those of us who were graduate students found that our teaching became a regular text in our seminars, a site we often wrote about, reflected on, and theorized. Here, teacher learning was ongoing, and everyone who sat around the table was (at least theoretically) positioned as at once a learner and a knower. Instead, then, of being trained, I was invited to participate in a process of pedagogical study and development.

To those of us in composition, these ideas are likely not altogether new or unique. After all, we work within a scholarly tradition that, as Sharon Crowley puts it, focuses on the "processes of learning rather than on the acquisition of knowledge" and a pedagogical tradition that emphasizes "change and development in students" rather than "transmission of a heritage" (1998, 3). It makes sense, then, that we have been prepared—and prepare graduate students—to participate in an ongoing process of teacher learning. But the notion of promoting teacher development as a central part of professorial preparation is still an anomaly in the larger discipline of English studies. Consequently, I write this book with those of us in composition—particularly graduate students like Mandi and those who teach them—in mind. I offer ways to reimagine our work with new teachers, as well as with full- and part-time colleagues, so as to promote pedagogical development and ongoing inquiry into what it means to profess English.

The Prominence of Pedagogy

Because of the prominence of "pedagogy" in and beyond our discipline, now seems like a particularly appropriate time to weigh in on how new conceptions of pedagogy might inform the way we prepare teachers of English. During the last decade, a growing body of work—largely informed by the language of radical pedagogy—has insisted that pedagogy not only be deemed as relevant an object of study as great authors or periods, but a subject with potential for social transformation. As a result, we now have a journal devoted to (and entitled) *Pedagogy* (from the prestigious Duke University Press), backed by an editorial board of pedagogy "scholars," and the *MLA International Bibliography* has expanded its scope to include "publications about the teaching of language, writing, and literature at the college level" ("Mellon Grant"). Though scholars disagree on the reasons for this "boom"—for instance, Gerald Graff (1994) contends that it results from an imperative to spell out critical theory's implications for teaching, while Lynn Worsham (1998) argues that it is driven by a recognition of the failures of theory to evoke social change—it has without question given a historically devalued subject new scholarly legitimacy.

But pedagogy has moved into the spotlight for more practical reasons, as well. More specifically, current job conditions create a renewed interest in "teacher training" and "professional preparation." An overproduction of Ph.D.s paired with a shortage of tenure-track positions means, according to the 2000 *MLA Newsletter* article "Job Market Remains Competitive," that 75 percent of job candidates will find positions at institutions that require them to spend most of their time teaching. This, of course, is an activity for which most Ph.D. recipients are ill prepared. Consequently, the MLA Committee on Professional Employment has recently urged graduate programs to revise doctoral education to better prepare graduate students for the realities of their future careers at teaching-centered institutions. So long as the research university devalues the teaching of lower-division courses, the committee warns, "graduate training will not adequately prepare students for the realities of the academic workplace" (40).

These trends might be read to suggest that teaching has gained the value and attention it has long deserved, and for which compositionists have long argued. However, the two primary ways in which these new pedagogical conversations take shape—scholarly, on one hand, and practical, on the other—suggest that it is not this simple. While making pedagogy a scholarly subject matter is indeed crucial, it does not necessarily alter the way in which pedagogy is engaged with students or the way doctoral candidates are prepared to teach. As I argue in Chapter 2, this scholarship on pedagogy tends to place its greatest emphasis on the theoretical tradition informing it (Marxism, feminism, poststructuralism, and so on), at the expense of attention both to specific instructional acts and to the particular students and teachers engaging them. As a result, questions of how we enact English studies with students in our classrooms, or how we learn to be professors of English, still often fall by the wayside as "practical"—not scholarly—concerns.

Alternatively, efforts that seek to institute "improved" teacher training practices—conversations which, in English studies, are found predominantly in composition—tend toward the "what works" or skills-based approaches (Latterell 1996; Haring-Smith 1985; Stenberg and Lee 2002) with a focus on teaching as a masterable craft rather than a site of critical inquiry. Considering the pressure WPAs are under to fill first-year composition classrooms, this should not be surprising.

More often than not, however, efforts toward "teaching improvement" are found outside the discipline in centers for excellence in teaching, programs such as Preparing Future Faculty, the Consortium on the Preparation of Graduate Students as College Teachers, and national TA conferences (Chism 1998). New methods of teacher preparation are also emerging, which include graduate student internships in community colleges and faculty-in-training programs (see, for example, Cowan, Traver, and Riddle 2001; Buck and Frank 2001; Murphy 2001). While these developments are important, they continue to relegate the job of teacher preparation to someplace outside of the doctoral curriculum, and thus to separate it from "real" scholarly work. Here reform is driven by the job market or the need for undergraduate teaching, not by a reconception of pedagogy as an important mode of knowledge production.

The problem, then, is that pedagogy is conceptualized either as a "subject matter" or a mere "practice." Either way, the result is the same: teaching is understood as a set of skills, not as an epistemic activity central to professorial work. I contend, then, that even as "pedagogy" has gained scholarly legitimacy and practical urgency, our conceptions of professing have not been sufficiently revised. Professing remains tied, primarily, to the production of research. Consequently, we have not seen a radical shift in how we facilitate pedagogical development for future professors of English.

Enacting Disciplinary (Re)visions: Rethinking Professing and Pedagogy

The central contention of *Professing and Pedagogy* is that efforts to improve the status of teaching or teacher development do little good when they do not also challenge deeply entrenched conceptions of the research professor and the discipline, which contribute to utilitarian conceptions of teaching. In Chapter 1, I argue that despite the field's recent lip service to pedagogy and the "teaching professor," we continue to abide by a model of the research professor imported from the German university around the turn of the last century. This professor was, in James Morgan Hart's words, "not a teacher" but a "specialist" committed, above all, to producing knowledge (quoted in Crowley 1998, 55). Though Hart's model has not gone unchallenged, it has also never been dismantled: research remains the professorial work that "counts," with teaching understood, although most often tacitly, as its by-product. This conception of the research professor is entangled with related notions of the discipline, conceived as a body of knowledge, with professors in charge of building and protecting it.

Ultimately, *Professing and Pedagogy* seeks to challenge the way we understand the role of the professor and the discipline in which he or she works. My method of revision reaches beyond providing new scholarly visions for pedagogy or improved "training" practices. Instead, I argue for a more holistic reform: to make pedagogy a central disciplined activity of English studies.

As I've suggested, pedagogy is an increasingly pervasive term in English studies. How it is used, however, varies tremendously; thus, it requires some unpacking here. Often, pedagogy is conflated with "teaching"—understood as the set of practices by which we transmit our knowledge. Other times, it is understood as the "theory" that informs teaching. Although I will define (and redefine) the term in each chapter, I want to foreground several key characteristics that shape my conception of pedagogy: (1) Pedagogy is a knowledge-making activity that involves the interplay of visions and practices, both of which require reflection; (2) pedagogy is dependent on learners and is remade with each encounter, as the students and the teacher change; (3) pedagogy cannot be finished; we cannot "finally" learn to teach. Rather, it requires an ongoing commit to learning and reflexivity (Lee 2000; Qualley 1997; Gallagher 2002; Kameen 2000).

If pedagogy is a collaborative activity that has to be remade every time a group of learners comes together, then the very notion that teachers can be *trained* unravels. Training, of course, implies the acquisition of an attainable skill. It assumes that a master will guide an apprentice down the path he or she determines most appropriate. It assumes learning will be one-way. Pedagogy, however, requires ongoing learning, study, and development. It is not something one can "pick up" in an orientation or even a single seminar. It is not something one can learn by observing an experienced pedagogue, or by reading.

Throughout this book, then, I will argue that instead of training teachers, those of us who locate ourselves in composition and rhetoric might take two actions: (1) teach new teachers to participate in a learning-centered discipline, and (2) invite our colleagues to engage in ongoing teacher-development opportunities. In this way, we can work to form collectives around pedagogy that help to alter our professorial work and foster disciplinary revision. After all, promoting pedagogy as intellectual work cannot, indeed should not, rest only on the shoulders of those of us in composition.

Some might ask (indeed, some readers of this manuscript have asked), "Why target compositionists? Isn't that just preaching to the choir? And don't we have enough work to do?" Maybe so, but I would contend that because it is compositionists who currently handle the pedagogical dimension of English studies, we are uniquely positioned to shape the people who will become (and teach) the next generation of English professors. Furthermore, as the field of composition becomes increasingly "disciplined," we need to be aware of our own tendencies to abide by the familiar research model, ensuring that we are not complicit in maintaining the low status of teaching in English.

Professing and Pedagogy seeks to promote this reconception of professing by offering both conceptual and instructional revisions. The book begins by providing a historical account of how entrenched notions of the discipline and the research professor have shaped the way we prepare teachers. Each subsequent chapter examines and critiques a root metaphor for the professor in training and the teacher-preparation methods that result, answering this material with both conceptual revisions and with specific institutional and pedagogical changes designed to influence how we understand and practice disciplinarity. This material does not come in the form of prescriptive or "how-to" advice, but offers illustrative examples of teachers and learners working together to engage pedagogical inquiry in specific contexts.

A Word about Form

In composing this book, I hope to avoid a tendency that afflicts much scholarship on pedagogy: favoring abstract social visions over inquiry into how students and teachers *enact* pedagogy. I take my cue from teacher-scholars Jennifer Gore, Elizabeth Ellsworth, Carmen Luke, and Mimi Orner, who have drawn from the ideas of critical pedagogy discourse but pushed for closer attention to the local, to the engagement of critical pedagogy with students. Luke and Gore, in their introduction to *Feminisms and Critical Pedagogy*, describe their work as a "political and social endeavor" to "distinguish this ongoing work in and through pedagogy from a generalized critical pedagogy" (1992, 1–2). Committed to feminist poststructuralist analysis, they argue that our work must foreground and attend to local contexts, so as to avoid the "'master's position' of formulating a totalizing discourse" (Orner 1992, 81). I hope to follow suit, showing the specific practices and processes through which professing and professorial development take place—rather than simply prescribing a "new" vision—in order to open possibilities for reflection and revision.

At the same time, however, I do not intend for my examples to serve as prescriptions or models. While new teachers who wonder, as I did, "How will I learn to teach?" and teacher "trainers" who want to know "How can I prepare TAs to teach?" may find ideas and strategies in this book, they will not find easy answers. Providing methods or "how to's" would only further reinforce the idea that teaching is a skill, not something that must be continually studied, reflected on, and revised within specific contexts. It would, in fact, run counter to my conception of pedagogy.

Instead of models, I offer both conceptual and instructional revisions. In so doing, I rely on a combination of theoretical and historical research, classroom narratives, and descriptions of specific programmatic and pedagogical practices. Just as I argue for teaching as a knowledge-producing site of inquiry, I hope to demonstrate that so, too, are classroom stories. As omnipresent as teacher narratives have become—particularly in the fields of composition and critical pedagogy—I am aware that, like teaching itself, they are often deemed intellectually suspect, considered merely anecdotal or illustrative. While they may be considered an acceptable way to demonstrate the *application* of theory, they tend not to be regarded as theory-generating. With Chris Gallagher, however, I approach teaching narratives not as "places for the 'practical' application, execution, and measurement of external, *a priori* theories," but as "sites of knowledge-production, where theory *happens*" (2002, 21). My hope, then, is that the dramatizations of teacher learning in each chapter will be read as sites of knowledge making, integral to the work of the chapter.

Of course, narratives can function in problematic ways. It becomes all too easy, I discovered in my composing process, to wrap these stories neatly and tightly so as to provide a "lesson," to tell the tale of moving from darkness into the light, to turn myself as narrator either into hero or antihero. But teacher learning is not linear or simple. Teacher learning has no ending. And so my goal is to represent this dynamic interchange of action and reflection, to show the ongoing process of the pedagogical inquiry I promote. I have worked to portray these stories as dynamic, fluid, and partial. I hope they serve not as answers, but as ongoing sites for reflection—to be made and remade, particularly as they work in dialogue with readers' own stories and insights.

A Look Ahead: Chapter Overview

So as to provide a fuller context for our contemporary "pedagogical boom" and its implications for professorial preparation, I spend the first two chapters examining the historical and current developments that shape this exigency. Chapter 1 examines three moments in the discipline's history when pedagogy emerged as a "boom" topic; consequently, scholars challenged the divide between teaching and professing and recommended reform of professorial preparation. My goal here is not to offer a comprehensive history of pedagogy in composition or English studies, but rather to focus on several "pedagogical turns" in the hope that they will offer insight into how efforts to value teaching have been disciplined, as well as to shed light on why particular metaphors for the teacher have so stubbornly endured in our institutional imaginations and practices.

Chapter 2 takes us from the historical to a closer look at the current scene, focusing on the metaphor of the "teacher as scholar." Here I consider the way two movements, critical pedagogy and the scholarship of teaching (Boyer 1990), have sought to legitimize pedagogy as a site of inquiry. I contend that despite the possibilities of each movement, they both tend to rewrite the teacher in the scholar's image and to reify the distinction between pedagogy (the subject) and teaching (the practice). While I argue that pedagogical scholarship is one important site for teacher learning, I suggest changes in the way we represent our teaching—focusing less on prescriptive visions or practical "how-to" approaches, and more on the local, specific engagement of pedagogical inquiry with students, so that we see a different kind of "teacher" in our scholarship.

In Chapter 3 I examine the "teacher-as-trainee" metaphor, whereby new teachers are positioned as blank slates whose pedagogical decisions follow from a single intellectual view provided by teacher-training programs. Instead, I seek to reconceive the teacher as a complex subject who brings a complicated pedagogical history to the classroom that is itself deserving of inquiry. New and experienced teachers alike, I contend, benefit from ongoing dialogue between the pedagogies from which we've learned and the pedagogies we aim to enact. To enact this argument, I narrate a complex moment in my history as a student, which is placed in dialogue with my responses as a teacher.

Chapter 4 explores the "teacher-as-owner" metaphor, whereby the classroom becomes the property of the teacher. Here professors are thought to develop in isolation, or in relationship to the scholarship they engage, rather than as a result of collaboration with other teachers. This chapter aims to challenge teaching as a privatized practice, and to promote a model of teacher learning that is equally dependent upon community and curriculum. I contend that if the work of developing teaching communities and curricula is understood as dialectical in relationship, the benefits reach not only the classrooms of individual teachers, but also the curriculum as a whole. Here I narrate the process of one teaching group, as we struggled to build and create community, and to negotiate our individual pedagogies in relation to a curriculum we worked to compose together. My intention is not to offer a prescription for teaching communities, but to dramatize the process of community building so that it might be studied and reflected upon. I also hope to show that while community must be negotiated, nurtured, and continually revised, it is indeed possible.

Finally, Chapter 5 puts together the revisionary ideas and behaviors offered in the previous chapters to argue for the "teacher as learner"—the professor who is committed to ongoing inquiry into his or her visions and practices with students and colleagues. Here I return to the discussion of discipline initiated in Chapter

1, this time examining and offering examples of how the discipline and our professorial practice would look with pedagogy at its center. Drawing from Richard Haswell's (1991) notion of writing development, I argue that true teacher development results in the change of the experienced teacher, the new teacher, and the field. Changing ourselves, then, means changing the discipline. Part of that change, however, must move beyond the conceptual and the pedagogical to alter the material realities we work within. In this chapter, I point to some of the material changes necessary if pedagogical development is to be given its due.

Ultimately, *Professing and Pedagogy* is not about critical answers but about critical processes: teaching, learning, questioning, collaborating, reflecting, revising. None of these are acts that can be finished. That is not the nature of pedagogy. It changes every moment, as students raise new questions, as a text causes discomfort, as silences or eruptions occur, as a learning moment fails (or succeeds) and we have to ask why, as a new group of student arrives and challenges what we thought we knew. This, to me, is also what makes professing such a rich, rewarding, exciting task: engaging and making knowledge with students, learning with and from them about what it means to profess English studies.

Teaching in the Research Model

It is the fall semester of 2003. My department works to revise a ten-year-old curriculum centered on periods of British and American literature, so as to better reflect current issues, concerns, and questions in the discipline. In part, this means including those subject areas that are now a sanctioned part of English: multicultural literature, gender studies, rhetoric and composition. But it also means asking how revising the content of our major will also require us to revise our pedagogies.

Recently, our talks have focused on our current gateway course Writing about Literature, which offers a solid introduction to the study and practice of literary criticism. But this can no longer be conflated with English studies, so the question becomes: how can we expand this course to introduce the field as it is currently configured? Ideally, several of us suggest, we would integrate the teaching and learning of literature and writing. To these ends, one of my colleagues provides a tentative sketch of gateway courses:

1. Interpreting Texts
   This course introduces students to theories of reading and composing. The texts at play will vary by professor, and may include established literary texts, underrepresented literary texts, creative writing, film, criticism, popular culture, rhetoric, etc. This course is designed to have students appreciate, by doing, the premise that all practice is equally informed by theory; and to have students begin to understand their own interpretive options and choices.

2. Entering a Professional Dialogue
   This course requires its students to enter a professional dialogue of their choice. This dialogue may pertain to any English-related topic—be it literary, critical, cultural, rhetorical, etc. This course will ask its beginning professionals to become familiar with the

scholarly resources that are most useful within their chosen fields, and to apply those resources toward the production of a piece of research composed with the goal of formally entering the dialogue in which it situates itself.

While these course ideas raise many interesting questions about the state of our field, what strikes me most is the shift of emphasis from literary texts or common theoretical critical approaches to a shared experience of producing knowledge with students. These courses, it seems to me, allow for a range of texts and theoretical schools, but they will not work without shared pedagogical goals. What these courses seem to imply, then, is that what matters most is pedagogy.

This shouldn't be surprising, since for the last twenty years, the field has (at least theoretically) taken what David Downing terms a "pedagogical turn," which shifts the focus from *what* we teach students to read and write to *how* we teach them (1994, xiii). Consequently, the role of the English professor is altered. More than one who transmits particular knowledge, he or she is a facilitator of student projects, a co-inquirer, a learner.

If we were to adopt these courses, we would need to give up the idea that our authority stems (solely) from our certainty, from the knowledge areas in which we have demonstrated achievement. After all, this pedagogy is not so much about transmission of predetermined knowledge as it is about the process of collaborative knowledge making, of asking questions, of learning. These courses require a commitment on the part of faculty to learn from their colleagues about other areas of the field and to learn with their students as they write their way into the field. But most of all, they require ongoing inquiry into how we are engaging knowledge with students, into how, as the Interpreting Texts description insists, "all [pedagogical] practice is equally informed by theory."

Of course, as Downing notes, "such reconsiderations will no doubt reveal that our uncertainties, our hesitancies, our vulnerabilities are a much larger part of the learning situation than our traditional notions of authority and knowledge have ever led us to believe" (xiv). Indeed, these course sketches were met with some discomfort on the part of faculty: how do we introduce students to areas of the field in which we are not experts? How can we help sophomore students locate appropriate projects? Do we teach creative writing as scholarly, and if so how? But perhaps we first need to address these questions: Do we know how to be the professors required by these descriptions, especially when so many of us in English studies were trained to be "masters" and not "learners"? Especially when so many of us were not trained as teachers, but as professors, scholars?

These issues and concerns are certainly not unique to my department; they have likely been felt to various degrees by most departments over the last twenty years as the infusion of cultural studies and critical theory into English studies has asked us to exchange foundational knowledge and transmission-based pedagogy for socially constructed knowledge and activity-centered learning. Certainly, this work has had an impact on the scholarship of English studies, resulting in a growing body of work examining the relationship between critical theory and classroom practices. What has not received nearly equivalent attention, however, is the issue of how we prepare professors of English to engage this new activity-centered field.

Addressing this issue is one aim of this book. But it can't be answered without a concurrent examination of historical and contemporary conceptions of the research professor and the discipline, notions that necessarily shape our beliefs about the relationship between teaching and research, the role of the professor, and the way he or she should be prepared. In this chapter, I begin by examining our current situation—what Gerald Graff has called the "pedagogical boom" (1994)—and the institutional and disciplinary conditions that gave rise to it. I then look to other historical moments when pedagogy has received heightened attention, so as to glean insight into the institutional structures and values that have disciplined, and continue to discipline, teaching. It is my hope that this sharpened understanding is a first step toward revision of the way we teach professors of English.

The Current Scene: A Turn toward Pedagogy

For those of us in composition, pedagogy has long occupied the center of our work. Rare is scholarship in composition that does not, implicitly or explicitly, address issues of teaching and learning. Of course, for this reason, the field has also been devalued and denied disciplinary status. As the field of English studies has begun to "turn" toward pedagogy, however, pedagogy's currency as a viable subject area has increased.

As I mention above, the collision of English, critical theory, and cultural studies has led to a new body of scholarship dedicated to issues, questions, and politics of pedagogy. For instance, in addition to numerous edited collections, we now have a journal devoted to (and entitled) *Pedagogy* (from the prestigious Duke University Press), backed by an editorial board of pedagogy "scholars," and, as noted earlier, the MLA *International Bibliography* has expanded its scope to include "publications about the teaching of language, writing, and literature at the college level" ("Mellon Grant").

This scholarship is largely informed by the language of radical (postmodern and critical) pedagogy, and has sought to establish pedagogy as what Henry Giroux calls "a mode of cultural criticism for questioning the very conditions under which knowledge and identities are produced" (1995, 6). Indeed, the pedagogical turn is fueled by the notion that pedagogy and politics are synonymous, and that pedagogy is crucial to social transformation. In fact, as Lynn Worsham (1998) sees it, pedagogy became a boom subject in the humanities when it became clear that theory, alone, was not doing the job. Pedagogy, with its ties to concrete sites and subjects, could fashion itself as a form of radical politics capable of changing (student) subjects, who could, in turn, change the world.

But how much has pedagogy changed English studies? Some would argue that despite the lip service, pedagogy is hardly a flourishing subject in our primary disciplinary sites: journals, conferences, book series. For instance, in their editors' introduction to the inaugural issue of *Pedagogy*, Jennifer L. Holberg and Marcy Taylor acknowledge significant pockets of interest (special issues of *PMLA, College English, Profession,* the MLA Approaches to Teaching series), but contend that pedagogy remains a marginalized subject in English studies at large. They describe sharing the journal's mission with others only to hear, "Oh, so it's a 'comp' journal." They argue, though, that not only is teaching not valued in the scholarship of literary study, it is also not valued in composition journals. As they write, "journals like *College Composition and Communication* are devoted to the scholarship of rhetoric and composition and not to teaching, any more than *Victorian Studies* is" (2000, 2).

Part of the problem is that scholarship on pedagogy is often more concerned with what Jennifer Gore calls the "social visions" than the "instructional acts" of teaching. That is, it typically remains at the level of abstract social visions, seemingly abiding by the assumption that someone else—namely the teachers—will unpack and deliver it to the students. In fact, Gore goes so far as to ask whether the new attention to pedagogy actually benefits students and teachers—whether it has actually reached classrooms. While it "dignifies" the work of educational theorizing, she is not so sure it has done much to dignify teaching itself (1993, 101).

Indeed, there seems to be a crucial distinction between pedagogy as it is written about in the scholarly realm and the actual practice of engaging English studies with students—the actual practice of *teaching*. This is evident when we examine the second (separate) way in which pedagogy has emerged as a "boom subject" in the field: as a response to the poor job market. As the 2000 *MLA Newsletter* article "Job Market Remains Competitive" makes clear, the combination of an overproduction of Ph.D.s and a shortage of tenure-track positions means that two-thirds of job candidates find themselves employed by institutions very different from the research universities where they did graduate work. They will, in other words, be required to spend a large percentage of their time teaching: an activity for which most recipients of Ph.D.s are ill prepared. As a result of this disjuncture, we see a renewed interest in "teacher training" and "professional preparation."

This interest has manifested itself largely in the development of programs that exist outside of any specific discipline, such as university-wide centers for excellence in teaching, programs such as Preparing Future Faculty, the Consortium on the Preparation of Graduate Students as College Teachers, and national TA conferences (Chism 1998). In the March 2001 issue of *Teaching English in the Two-Year College*, essays by Jo Ann Buck and

MacGregor Frank; Toni Cowan, Joyce Traver, and Thomas Riddle; and Sean Murphy offer new possibilities for preparing doctoral students as teachers, including graduate student internships in community colleges and faculty-in-training programs. While these programs make important contributions, they also demonstrate that teaching is not considered a disciplinary concern; it can somehow be amputated from scholarly issues and handed over to others for whom it is presumably more properly an object of inquiry. Even more, reform is driven by the job market or the need for undergraduate teaching, not by a reconception of pedagogy as an important mode of knowledge production.

Within the discipline of English studies, we might expect professorial preparation to look somewhat different. That is, if pedagogy is truly deemed a crucial mode of knowledge production deserving of critical inquiry, then we should see evidence of a radical departure from the very concept of teacher *training*, which suggests that teaching is a skill one can acquire or master. But there is much to suggest the contrary. For starters, the responsibility for preparing graduate students to teach typically falls on one person: the writing program administrator. Often, this training is completed during a brief orientation or a single "teaching seminar" or "practicum." (There are exceptions, of course: many innovative courses and programs that support teacher development do exist, and I will draw from these examples here and in subsequent chapters to illustrate how the ideas I promote can be enacted.)

Because of institutional pressure to move new TAs into classrooms as quickly and efficiently as possible, the overwhelming majority of teacher-training programs still rely on "what-works" or skill-based methods to prepare new teachers, according to Catherine Latterell, who studied curricular requirements for TAs in thirty-six universities that grant Ph.D.s in rhetoric and composition studies (1996, 27). In this moment when English studies calls attention to the contexts of knowledge—to the importance of studying the social relations that inform how and what we come to know—it is ironic that "what works" teacher-training strategies, expected to function devoid of contexts, continue to function as the norm.

On the other hand, we are beginning to see an increasing number of theory-based courses, many of which serve at once to introduce students to the discipline of composition and rhetoric and to prepare TAs to teach first-year writing. There is nothing inherently problematic about offering TAs either "what works" practices or composition theory; both, in fact, are necessary. What is worth noting, however, is how teacher-preparation sites tend to feature one or the other, following disciplinary trends in making pedagogy either a body of knowledge or a skill.

Further, this preparatory work is not often designed to initiate the career-long development of graduate students, but to answer immediate program requirements. Consequently, teaching is often only addressed when it serves the needs of the university. In doctoral programs (or, more accurately, outside of them), then, graduate students learn that teaching may be important to subsidize their "real" work, but that it is not central to their development as professors. Of course, this lesson begins upon admittance to graduate school: graduate students teaching first-year writing courses are almost exclusively admitted for doctoral study based not on their potential as teachers, but their potential as scholars. What matters most is that which is emphasized in their credit-bearing courses: scholarly development.[1]

Because of the job crunch, however, there has been increasing pressure to professionalize graduate students, and to help them represent their teaching in ways that increase their marketability (Leverenz and Goodburn 1998, 13). While the development of teaching portfolios offers important opportunities for reflection and revision, teaching portfolios created for the purpose of self-promotion differ greatly from those composed for teaching development; likewise, as Carrie Shively Leverenz and Amy Goodburn point out, they are not typically assessed in "terms of growth or development but in the degree to which teachers represent themselves as successful" (13). Once again, teaching is granted attention not because of its inherent value as a subject matter, but because it is a vehicle for job placement.

As much as the recent pedagogical boom has helped recast pedagogy as a site of scholarly study and illuminated the need for better teacher preparation, there is much to suggest that it is already disciplined. Put simply, this movement does one of two things: it turns pedagogy into a "new" body of knowledge or it reifies the notion that pedagogy is merely a skill, subsidiary to the real, disciplinary work that takes place in the curriculum. Valuing pedagogy, making pedagogy central to professing, requires more than scholarly efforts and more than improved training practices. It requires a rethinking of entrenched notions of the discipline that determine the relationship of teaching to scholarship and that reinforce a limited conception of who the professor is and should be.

Disciplining the Research Professor

To explore our contemporary conceptions of the discipline, and the research professor who occupies it, we need to look all the way back to the German research university. When the United States adopted this model at the turn of the last century, university education shifted away from its service-oriented mission and uniform curriculum, whose aim was to produce "public-spirited, service-oriented" graduates (Kuklick 1990). Instead, it embraced the German ideal of *Wissenschaft,* which promoted, above all, the "ardent, methodical, independent search after truth in any and all of its forms, but wholly irrespective of utilitarian application" (Hart 1874, 250). Under this new research ideal, students were free to elect new courses of study, at the same time American professors were freed from accountability to their students (Crowley 1998; Berlin 1987). Their new responsibility was to knowledge. As James Morgan Hart, an American who traveled in 1861 to Germany to study, put it, "[T]he professor is not a teacher, in the English sense of the term; he is a specialist. He is not responsible for the success of his hearers. He is responsible only for the quality of his instruction. His duty begins and ends with himself" (1874, 264).

The new research university also gave way to a new conception of disciplinarity, conceived as a static body of specialized (not utilitarian) knowledge, made and extended by "experts" and transported by "teachers." This transition, Richard Ohmann reminds us, was steered by the "unseen hand that guides a laissez faire economy" (1976, 288). That is, the new research-driven discipline was easily appropriated to serve the goals of scientific management (Downing, Hurlbert, and Mathieu 2002). As Downing (2002) argues, one of the most significant consequences of these corporate appropriations was teaching's subordination to research. Put simply, disciplinary knowledge could be more easily quantified and commodified than could teaching.

The development of doctoral education in English, beginning in the early twentieth century, also helped to cement English as a research discipline and to establish what Stephen North calls "College English Teaching, Inc." Under this structure, doctoral students contributed to the university economy through both their tuition dollars and their labor, payments that ultimately served to maximize graduate faculty's profits as researchers. By acting as teaching fellows or assistants, doctoral students would generate credit hours at a fraction of the price of full-time faculty (2000, 25). Moreover, these teaching duties were considered ancillary to credit-bearing, disciplinary work; at most, teaching might have been considered an extracurricular "apprenticeship." Under this model, the students were subjected not only to the "master's" instruction, but also to his rule. After all, as North writes, "when the faculty from whom you are seeking your education are also in charge of your means of funding that education, they can exercise more control—and more direct control—over the trajectory it follows than faculty without that fiscal power" (27).

The payoff was great for graduate faculty, who, now excused from teaching labor-intensive lower-level classes, could dedicate more time to the disciplinary work of researching. When they did teach, it was typically in their research areas (and enrollments could be guaranteed through graduate course requirements). Thus, the link between professing and knowledge mastery was confirmed, as was the notion that the labor of teaching could be handed over to someone "lower" on the academic totem pole. Indeed, the work of teaching became something quite different from the work of professing. Teaching was crucial in making the disciplinary machine run, but it functioned in service of—not as central to—that machine.

But I need not use the past tense here. This model, institutionalized in American universities more than a century ago, remains largely predominant in academia today, and is so entrenched as to be rendered natural, invisible.[2] In fact, as James Slevin examines current conceptions of disciplinarity, his description bears a striking resemblance to the discipline undergirding Hart's model:

> A discipline is currently understood as the knowledge of a given field of study, the intellectual skill and labor required for the making of that knowledge, and the disciplinary community in conversation with one another about it. It is conceptualized as a spatial object, with perimeters that contain a specialized knowledge, method, and dialogue. Disciplines are thus defined by their boundaries, and distinguished membership in the discipline, not to mention tenure and promotion, can be gained only be extending these boundaries, almost always in an agonistic relationship to others engaged in similar work. This boundary-breaking *agon* happens well apart from those excluded, those who are not—or not yet—so engaged. (1996, 155–56)

Those excluded, of course, are graduate and undergraduate students, as well as those part-time teachers and TAs who fuel the disciplinary "economy." Given this conception of disciplinarity, it makes sense that professors are still prepared first and foremost to produce scholarship in isolation, rather than to engage knowledge with others.

Even as the pedagogical turn has encouraged us to ask how we engage English studies with students, it hasn't dramatically changed the way we prepare professors of English or increased the value we place on the praxis of teaching. Nor has it changed the divisions of labor whereby we separate those who teach from those who profess (with the former supporting the latter). As Michael Murphy contends, in the last fifteen years American universities have increasingly moved toward a system that "subsidizes their research faculty by creating what [his] part-time colleague, Henry Jankiewicz, calls a stable, reliable *teaching substructure*" (2000, 22–23). The numbers show as much: a 1998 MLA report indicates that in Ph.D.-granting departments, TAs teach 63 percent of first-year writing sections, part-timers 19 percent, and full-time non-tenure-track faculty members 14 percent. Given the distinction between the behaviors known as professing and those known as teaching, then, it is not surprising that learning to profess has historically been—and remains—an altogether different process from learning to teach.

Of course, it isn't to say that this exigency, this divide between teaching and professing, has not been felt before—far from it. A look back over nearly a century's worth of English journals demonstrates a long history of teacher-scholars struggling to challenge the seemingly naturalized breakdown between teaching and research, insisting that we need not only to improve teaching at the university level, but also to value it as central to the professor's work. That is to say, the history of English studies has experienced several "pedagogical turns." I move now to examine these "turns," since they offer us insight into how efforts to value teaching have been disciplined; they further demonstrate how long limiting metaphors for the teacher have existed, and how stubbornly they remain in our institutional imaginations. These constraints need to be challenged if new conceptions of professing are to develop.

The Post–World War II Pedagogical Turn

It could be argued that the first "pedagogical turn" in English studies occurred after World War II, when—thanks to the GI Bill, the booming war economy, increased federal support for higher education, and the civil rights movement—undergraduate enrollments increased by more than 50 percent (North 2000, 43). Not surprisingly, this boom in undergraduate education contributed to a similar increase in doctoral programs in English. While this growth was in part due to a growing number of English undergraduates with an interest in pursuing advanced degrees, the need for more university professors to teach the growing student body also contributed to rising Ph.D. production (44). In fact, Don Cameron Allen's 1968 report entitled *The Ph.D. in English and American Literature* warned the public and the profession of the increasing gap between the demand for qualified university teachers in English and the number of Ph.D.s granted. Allen, relying on the predictions of government experts, believed that this growth would pose a problem for a field ill-prepared to handle the projected nine million students (and eighty thousand sections of first-year composition) entering the university by 1975. While this wouldn't be the case—and, as North puts it, "more than one generation of un- and under-employed Ph.D. holders would pay dearly for [the field's] excesses"—one effect of this feared shortage of teachers was increased attention granted to issues of teacher preparation (42).

Indeed, according to Janet Marting's "Retrospective on Training Teaching Assistants," the early to mid-1960s produced a "tremendous amount" of professional interest in the training of college English teachers, reflected in an explosion of conference papers and publications on TA training (1987, 37).[3] Out of sheer necessity, pedagogy became a "boom subject" in the discipline of English.

Of course, increased volume of pedagogical conversations means little if the tone and pitch of these conversations do not change, as well. Allen's project, which surveyed department chairs as to how the field should produce "qualified" teachers, reveals the field's disposition regarding teacher preparation. The majority of chairs surveyed, 67 percent, wanted to answer the need for teachers by creating an alternative teaching degree; the majority, that is, wanted to preserve the Ph.D. as a research degree (203).

Those who expressed interest in improving teacher preparation within doctoral programs supported one of two approaches: some relied on the familiar argument that better scholarship would "naturally" produce better teaching; others wanted to incorporate teacher training into the doctoral curriculum. The first proposal relies on the familiar belief that, as one respondent put it, "a Ph.D. improves the odds that a man will be a better teacher" (77). This is perhaps our most deeply entrenched metaphor: the professor as scholar, whereby good professing has more to do with the relationship one has to knowledge than to students. It was important for those on this side of the debate, then, to distinguish their professorial work from what *teachers* did. As one respondent argued, "[I]f they want teachers, why don't they hire teachers?" (77). While the professor was thought to be a knowledge maker, one who brings a particular "quality" product to the classroom, the teacher was merely the transmitter of knowledge produced by someone else. The Ph.D. seemingly served as a guarantee that one was committed to *making,* not merely *transmitting,* knowledge.

On the other hand, those who argued that teaching must be part of doctoral education insisted, as some in Allen's study did, that "there is practically no connection between graduate training and the lifetime task of teaching generation after generation of undergraduates" (77). Administrators on this side of the debate put pressure on the well-institutionalized binary privileging research over teaching, arguing that the professor's commitment must move beyond his own scholarly work to encompass the students he teaches. Halio makes a similar case in his 1964 *College English* article, claiming that part of the aim of teacher training must be to "awaken our fledgling colleagues to the fact that their responsibilities go somewhat further than establishing themselves as scholars, critics, and overpowering young polymaths" (226). In his recommendation to doctoral programs, Allen echoes this sentiment, arguing, "The Ph.D. [. . .] is assumed to possess a broad knowledge of his subject and the ability to explore and interpret. [. . .] Too often the emphasis is on exploring it and interpreting it in a way sufficient to himself and to like-minded specialists when, if we may say it again, his honest professional duty is to the undergraduate student" (117).

Other reform-minded scholars agreed, calling attention to the problems that stem from the assumption that good teaching is the by-product of good research. As Don Cook contended, graduate students too often assume that a "set of meticulous notes from a good course in the Victorian novel" is adequate preparation for teaching the same course. This model tended to render invisible the pedagogy through which one learned, such that "the way [the student] was taught is the way to teach; [. . .] the synthesis offered by his professor is inevitable" (1965, 114). Students didn't "see" how they were taught, because the pedagogy was assumed to be a neutral vehicle for transmitting the content. By contrast, Cook argued that more consideration must be granted to teaching methods, and that teacher training must become an integral component of doctoral education.

In order to learn more about established teacher-training practices as well as efforts to improve new professors' teaching, John Jordan (1965) surveyed English department chairs from 436 colleges and universities. His results demonstrated that the most "fruitful" (and common) method of teacher training was simply using advanced graduate students as teachers. (He notes, however, that this is not often "formally recognized" as practice teaching since "nobody likes to be practiced on" [113]). Not surprisingly, the most common course that graduate assistants taught was first-year writing, a course that, as Cook puts it, gives the TA a diet on which to "cut his teeth" before moving to the "occasional treats" of literature courses (115). Other established practices included assisting regular faculty members by reading papers or delivering the occasional lecture (110). Jordan found that fewer than 14 percent surveyed used classroom observations, and this occurred most regularly at large universities where "there are large numbers of faculty to be assimilated and reviewed" (112). Generally speaking, then, the most nearly universal "training" practice was simply to put new teachers in classrooms, and to assume that experience was sufficient.

Other models did exist, however. At Indiana University TAs were used to staff "elementary" composition classes, but were also required to enroll in a course dubbed "the roundtable" (Cook 1965, 116). In the roundtable, new TAs discussed with the director of composition methods, assignments, and grading practices. Assessment came in the form of observation, and the resulting report determined the teacher's next assignment and whether he or she was in need of a subsequent visit. These practices, and the assumptions informing them, are familiar enough, and here we see another metaphor that remains deeply entrenched: the teacher as "trainee" or "apprentice." Teaching is conceived as a set of practices or skills—writing assignments, grading papers, lecturing—that can presumably be applied in any given classroom, with any students. The administrator or "master" teacher observes the TA to assess whether the appropriate skills have been acquired, whether the TA has adequately assimilated the particular program's pedagogical goals and values. Once these goals are accomplished, no further observations are required: the reward is "freedom" or isolation. While this model assumes that teaching requires more preparation than traditional scholarly work, it also separates teacher learning from scholarly acquisition—a division that remains in our contemporary doctoral programs.

Indiana University also relied upon a more innovative method, which was described at the time as "still highly experimental." Instead of separating teacher training from the curriculum, the program invited doctoral students to take a series of credit-bearing courses, which led to a minor in the teaching of college English. The sequence required students to take one course each in the teaching of composition and of literature. As part of this coursework, they were positioned as "apprentices," expected to observe various teachers' classrooms, help grade examinations and papers, and prepare lectures and "lesson plans" (Cook 1965, 117).

The latter two courses comprised a survey of the study of English literature, intended to give the doctoral student a "thorough grasp of his profession," and a capstone entitled "Assumption and Practice in the Teaching of English," designed to help the doctoral student "bring to bear on his teaching the principles, methods and perspectives derived from the prior survey" (118). Here particular emphasis was placed on "the contribution that the critical, biographical, and editorial techniques developed since 1900 can make to the teaching of specific texts" (118). The course required students to select two or three pieces of literature to discover what was "revealed" when various approaches were employed. Then, they were to select an author and prepare a series of lectures exploring his or her work through alternative methods (118).

Ultimately, then, the course was concerned less with pedagogy (the method of delivery, lecture, is taken as a given), and more with providing doctoral students an occasion to apply various modes of literary analysis to texts. That is, textual approaches were conflated with pedagogical approaches, so that the teacher was positioned as scholar: better teaching was the result of the professor's improved ability to analyze texts. While questions may have been asked about how the text changed depending on one's approach to it, the classroom—no matter what literary application was engaged—remained the same. The pedagogy depended primarily on the teacher as scholar—on the interaction between the text and the (soon-to-be) professor, not the professor and the students. So while this mode of reform at least located concerns of teaching within the curriculum, it ultimately reinforced the notion that teaching is a mode of delivering the professor's (finished) knowledge. The metaphor, teacher as scholar, remains.

While the aim of each of these reform efforts was to improve teaching practices, none of them significantly challenged the institutional structure that devalues teaching. Whether focusing on better scholarly preparation, improved training practices, or new textual approaches, the new practices and training models were finally designed to improve—not overhaul—the institutional model that was in place. As a result, modifications were made, but the role of the professor—whether serving as a model to TAs or delivering knowledge to students—remained largely untouched.

Preserving the Research Degree: Reform through the Doctor of Arts

Considering the endurance of the research model and the model of the research professor that accompanies it, it is not surprising that the most popular response (67 percent) to Allen's survey was to create an alternative degree that emphasized teaching, ultimately preserving the Ph.D. for research and scholarly activity. Options for this new degree ranged from "restoring" the master's degree as the essential qualification for college teaching (1968, 28) to creating an "intermediate" degree granted either to those who had completed all of the Ph.D. requirements except for the dissertation or who had an interest in teaching more than research (29). Since there were an abundance of holders of ABDs at this time, degrees like the master of philosophy developed at Yale in 1966 were intended to legitimize this educational status and to "dethrone" the Ph.D. as the only degree that allowed one a university teaching position (28–29).

Though one college chairman argued that "the Ph.D. training should have teaching requirements and those who show no ability as teachers should be denied the degree" (80), the fact that so many respondents favored the implementation of alternative teaching degrees (which were understood as lower in status than the Ph.D.) seems to point instead to a desire to *deny* the Ph.D. to those who valued teaching over or alongside scholarship. Indeed, the doctor of arts degree was established in response to a need for teachers—for increased "service"—and was thus set up institutionally to function as the pragmatic "other" to the research-based Ph.D. Even so, the development of the D.A. offered a compelling vision for making pedagogy a central part of a doctoral curriculum. D.A. programs took suggestions like Cook's "minor in the teaching of English"—intended to make teaching a component of doctoral study—one step further, by making teaching integral to one's course of study.

One such effort is represented in Kenneth Eble's 1972 description of Carnegie-Mellon's doctor of arts degree. In imagining possibilities for reforming Ph.D. programs, as well as working to build momentum for more doctor of arts programs, Eble strives to overturn the teaching-research binary by privileging teaching as "high art." In doing so, he argues that we must work against many dominant assumptions about teaching:

> [We must challenge] the belief that the inherent worth of subject matter makes it unnecessary to work at the teaching of it; that the purity of the truth scholars pursue, the objectivity of the scholarly method, rules against a personal involvement in teaching; that pedagogical concerns are to be left to education departments; that truly gifted teachers are born, not made; and that satisfactory teaching can be done by almost anyone who knows enough about his subject. (386)

Eble also works to disrupt the notion that teaching is distinct from scholarship and therefore not worthy of study. He is concerned that training is usually equated with coursework, formal research, and dissertation production in one's field of specialty. And when coursework in teaching was being offered, he points out, "it often appears to be an outgrowth of specific needs of teachers of freshman composition, and aimed more at the assistant teaching in the institution in which he is taking graduate work than at the prospective faculty member elsewhere" (393). Teacher training, then, functioned primarily to serve the university in which one is a graduate student, not to promote one's ongoing development as a teacher-scholar.

Eble proposed several ideas for making pedagogy a crucial part of the doctoral curriculum, pointing to the doctor of arts degree at Carnegie-Mellon as a site where these ideas were already being enacted. First, while he noted that Ph.D. students benefit from firsthand teaching experience, he argued for limiting the number of courses graduate students teach. His argument is important and historically unique in its effort to make visible the way in which universities tended to exploit TA labor. He writes, "until a department is willing and able to break the connection between economic necessity and the employment of graduate students, the training of graduate students as teachers will be less than it should be" (400). Second, he argued that the faculty's support of new teachers must be strengthened and deemed a worthwhile use of resources. He suggested using faculty to co-teach lower-division classes with graduate students, not to replicate the familiar master-apprentice model but to serve as a "valuable learning experience for both parties" (401).

More than his contemporaries, Eble was interested not only in adding "better" practices, but also in revising the conceptual underpinnings of practices already in place. For instance, he called for the use of classroom visits, but proposed that they need not be only a means of "checking on" new teachers but of "developing interest and effectiveness of both the visitor and the visited" (401). Here, the assumption is that the visiting professor is still developing, and might even have something to learn from the new teacher. Not only does this challenge the master-apprentice model, but it also makes the professor an ongoing learner who benefits from a relationship to both scholarship and to other teachers. In this way, Eble disrupted the deeply rooted metaphor of "teacher as apprentice," promoting instead the professor as learner.

Eble also argued that traditional coursework might be considered part of teacher preparation if professors took responsibility for highlighting the connections among scholarship, teaching, and learning. In the ideal graduate program, he wrote, "every subject matter course would be a course in pedagogy" (401). In other words, he saw it as the professor's responsibility to render visible the choices he or she made in engaging knowledge with others; his or her primary responsibility is not solely to the body of knowledge, but also to his or her pedagogy, and to those who experience it. Finally, Eble suggested that the dissertation, which currently offered no evidence of a candidate's ability to engage his or her scholarship with others, must be rethought. In this way, he disrupted the notion that scholarly "capabilities" can be conflated with the ability to teach. In fact, by making this statement, he questioned our very definition of research. Quite often, research is privileged *because* of its lack of connection to the "practical." Instead, Eble promotes a form of research that works in dialectical relation to one's teaching.

In arguing for a doctoral program that values teacher development within its curriculum, Eble points to two programs offering D.A.s at the time—the University of Utah and Carnegie-Mellon University. He saw both as valuing pedagogical investigation alongside traditional scholarly research. For instance, at Carnegie-Mellon, the candidate's thesis (taking the place of a dissertation) could take three forms: curricular, scholarly, or creative. No matter which form was chosen, however, the project was required to take into consideration its implications for teaching and learning:

> Each will relate literary scholarship to the teaching of literature. That is, the dissertation based primarily on curricular or pedagogical research will be consonant with sound scholarship and criticism of the literature involved, and the dissertation based primarily on historical or critical research will examine the implications of its findings for teaching. (403)

While the teacher-training practices discussed in the section above tended to make teaching a skill-based add-on to professorial work, Eble's representation of the D.A. encompasses exactly the kind of revisionary work that has potential to move beyond mere reform. Instead of simply donating more time to improving teaching methods, the D.A. programs he describes refused to sever teaching from disciplinary or scholarly work. He seems, in fact, to be suggesting in 1972 what many social-turn scholars would argue in the late 1980s and early 1990s: that questions of what we teach and learn cannot be separated from how we do so.

Of course, the factors that ultimately constrained the doctor of arts degree should not be ignored. Most notably, this degree was designed as an alternative to the research degree, presumed to relieve the Ph.D. of its responsibilities to teaching, thereby hindering its possibilities of radically altering the conception of the professor's work. The D.A.'s potential was also squelched by the fact that Allen's predictions were wrong. English as an under-graduate major did not experience the growth he predicted. In fact, interest in English reached a peak in the mid-1960s, gently declined through the end of that decade, and fell sharply through the 1970s (North 2000, 48). Fewer majors meant fewer profes-sors were needed to teach them, and this decline eventually helped to produce what North calls the "Great Contraction," which led to a "nightmarish job market crunch" during the late 1970s and early 1980s (50). Without a need for teachers, there was not a need for the doctor of arts degree. The possibilities arising from the pedagogical boom of the great expansion were thus seriously constrained,[4] finally demonstrating that teaching became impor-tant to the field primarily because teachers were needed, not be-cause the status quo—the Ph.D. as a research degree—was thought to be problematic.

Process Pedagogy and Professionalization: Another Pedagogical Turn

Though the "Great Contraction" contributed to a significant decrease of English majors, and limited the job prospects of those pursing advanced degrees in English, it did not, as North argues, result in a simple reversal of the "Great Expansion" (2000, 51). In fact, the sixties and seventies proved to be times of dramatic growth for overall undergraduate enrollment in universities, thanks largely to the growing size of the student-age population and the expanding corporate and state sectors of the economy (Berlin 1987). During the sixties, colleges became "training cen-ters" for the new specialists needed in business and government, and thus, "their power, prestige, size, and numbers increased" (120). It was the collision of these two factors—increased stu-dent populations and emphasis on specialized training—that helped open a door for compositionists to make their work, and subsequently, issues of pedagogy, visible. Ironically, then, the Great Contraction led to yet another surge of pedagogical interest.

It played out something like this. First, universities experi-enced pressure to offer more service courses to meet the needs of the growing, and increasingly diverse, student body. As a result, first-year writing boomed. These service classes were largely relegated to non-tenure-track instructors and TAs, who provided inexpensive labor, and—because of the job market crunch—many Ph.D.s at this time found themselves hired into positions where they would teach lower-division service courses to nonmajors, courses that had little or nothing to do with their areas of expertise (North 2000). On the one hand, this development reinforced the low status of undergraduate teaching, and especially of writing "service" courses; presumably, these courses could be taught by anyone, no matter his or her training or interests. On the other hand, the sheer numbers of undergraduates needing writing instruction made concerns of writing pedagogy more visible—and more urgent—giving compositionists leverage to argue for graduate training in their field, and to promote their professional status (Berlin 1987).

No academic specialty, of course, is admitted disciplinary entry without a ticket: a demonstrable body of knowledge. Though composition teachers had long centered their professional attention on developing and maintaining first-year writing, this changed around 1971, when process pedagogy provided the research base necessary to argue that composition teachers had a tangible site of study—the composing processes of student writers (Crowley 1998, 195). Compositionists could then make the case that not just anyone could teach writing—special *scholarly* training in composition and rhetoric was needed. Now, composition could claim a subject to be professed, not merely taught.

The development was also aided by another rather surprising result of the "Great Contraction." In English studies, even as the number of Ph.D.s decreased, the number of *programs* offering the degree increased (North 2000, 51). As programs competed with one another to attract students, more specializations were offered. The timing was just right for composition. While no English department offered a doctorate with a primary emphasis in composition, by the end of the 1980s, about two dozen programs "served a job market featuring plenty of positions calling for just this specialization" (54).

The combination of greater attention to first-year writing courses and a growing visibility of composition meant increased

attention to the preparation of teachers. With empirical and theoretical evidence that writing and its teaching could be and deserved to be studied, issues of teacher training reemerged in
composition scholarship. Significantly, teaching was no longer
discussed purely in skill-based terms; rather, it became a site of
study, and an art that one could develop and hone.

Peter Elbow's "The Definition of Teaching" (1968) provides
a compelling early example of pedagogical visions made possible
by process thinking. Here Elbow critiques the model of teaching
whereby knowledge is acquired apart from students and then
transported to them by the professor. Instead, he envisions teaching as a process of asking new questions *with* students, such that
a "spirit of questioning, wondering, and doubting" is central.
Elbow's argument is historically important in its attempt to disrupt the entrenched model privileging research over teaching,
mastery over inquiry, and product over process (191). In fact,
Elbow argues that the most productive learning situations occur
when the teacher is not an expert in his or her field but is learning along with the students. For this reason, he insists that positioning graduate students as "once-a-week section men trying to
pick up the pieces of another man's course" is a waste of the
interest and energy new teachers bring to a learning situation
(195). Elbow thus builds on Eble's metaphor of the "professor as
learner," arguing that teachers can learn from students, and experienced "master" teachers can learn from new teachers, because the aim of education is not to transmit and acquire
knowledge, but to ask questions and participate in collaborative
discovery.

A look to the literature on teacher training during the era
shows evidence of reform in this direction; new importance was
placed on exchanging the master-apprentice model, which assumes that teaching is a skill one can finally learn, with a process
approach, valuing teaching as an ongoing developmental course.
Conceptions of teacher evaluation were among the first to undergo critical scrutiny. Just as process writing pedagogy sought
to eliminate the "red pen" of current-traditionalism, favoring
instead the creation of a supportive atmosphere in which writers
could thrive, process-oriented teacher training emphasized a supportive and nonjudgmental relationship intended to enable the

new teacher to discover his or her "style," rather than to imitate or assume that of a more experienced or "master" teacher.

This new conceptualization of supportive relationships between new and experienced teachers is evidenced in the revision of traditional practices such as classroom visits. Instead of acting as surveillance mechanisms, visits were intended to provide new teachers increased "awareness" of what was happening in their classrooms. Gene Krupa argues in his 1982 article "Helping New Teachers of Writing: Book, Model, and Mirror" that experienced teachers should serve not as evaluators, but as "mirrors," reflecting the new teacher's classroom in a nonevaluative way. Reflection was here a device that would show new teachers a fuller picture of their classrooms since, as Krupa claims, "our identity as teachers is a function of *the quality of our awareness* of what is happening in our classrooms" (443). If new teachers could see their choices more clearly, with help from their "mirrors," then they could decide for themselves where revision was necessary.

In addition to challenging the evaluative relationship between experienced and new teachers, process methods also emphasized collaborative learning among new teachers. In fact, in their 1984 article "The Socialization of Writing Teachers," Lil Brannon and Gordon Pradl requested that new teachers form groups to share their own writing—enacting themselves the same kind of practices their students would later be engaging. Besides asking these teachers to experience, in a sense, their own pedagogies—something uncommon in a research model in which the students' experience matters little—they also sought to enable a sense of community among teachers. This posed a significant challenge to a model that has traditionally encouraged teachers to retreat to isolated classrooms, consulting other teachers (usually experienced ones) only if problems arise. Instead, Brannon and Pradl suggested that teachers could learn about teaching by engaging, as learners, together. In fact, the thrust of their argument was that new teachers benefit from positioning themselves as learners. To this end, one of the central practices Brannon and Pradl promoted involved inviting new teachers to reflect on their own writing processes, and their histories as student writers. For them, the aim of teacher training was to help teachers "redefine themselves [. . .] on the basis of who they are as writers" (28).

As these examples demonstrate, process-oriented writing pedagogy and teacher training practices provided a new metaphor, one that will be promoted throughout this book: the teacher as learner. At the same time, they promoted a curious blend of learning via collaboration and individual exploration. That is, the primary aim of collaborative activities was to help each participant discover and enhance his or her own inherent "style," whether as a writer or as a teacher. For instance, in his 1977 *CCC* Staffroom Interchange, William Coles argues that the pedagogy of teacher training should be no different from the pedagogy of the writing classroom; if teachers of writing are to enable students to "develop voices or styles of their own [. . .] then it would seem reasonable to suppose that our primary responsibility in the training of teachers to teach writing is to provide them with the same opportunity" (268). For Coles, the aim of teacher training was not to provide a set of assumptions or methods for how writing *should* be taught—which would only reinforce the master-apprentice dynamic—but to foster a "teacher's belief in his or her assumptions" and a "commitment to his or her methods" (270).

Of course, as social-turn scholars (to use John Trimbur's term) have made clear, process—and particularly expressivist—pedagogy tends to rely on modernist assumptions of the individual, whereby the locus of power is inside each person. Likewise, process-expressivist teacher-training practices sometimes assumed a latent teaching style within, which one could—with the help of a nurturing mentor—discover and develop. While the notion that development is an organic, inner process of discovering one's unique and authentic "style" represented a step away from the master-apprentice model, it left little room for examining the social contexts informing those processes and selves. In fact, power differentials—between student and teacher and among students—tended, at least in these representations, to be overlooked.

Further, while process practices encouraged the collaboration of new and experienced teachers, the intended result was to aid each other in becoming better *individual* (and thus separate) teachers. That is, the sanctity of individual ideas, beliefs, and assumptions was ultimately preserved, so that "difference" was acknowledged only as contributing to a comfortable pluralism, where everyone was entitled to his or her own style. Here we see another predominant metaphor: teacher as owner of pedagogy. Teaching became "private property," the domain of a single teacher behind a closed door (Gallagher, Gray, and Stenberg 2002).

The tendency of process-expressivist approaches to preserve the "individual" functioned, in turn, to preserve the research professor. Though teaching became a process that one could study and reflect on with the aid of others, the notion that one's teaching style is buried "within" reinforced the idea that discovery of knowledge (or pedagogy) ultimately occurs at the individual level. Just as the professor retreats to his study to discover knowledge, the teacher retreats within to discover her pedagogical style. Once she does, she is presumably finished—or, she might continue to work on honing this style on her own. The latter notion is reinforced by the fact that in process-based teacher training scholarship, development seemingly remained an endeavor associated with "new" teachers. While it should follow—especially since there is so much attention given during this moment to disrupting master-apprentice relationships—that *all* teachers should engage in teacher-learning activities, nowhere did I find these practices suggested for experienced teachers.

During this "turn," we also see elements of the teacher as scholar, particularly as composition worked to establish itself as a legitimate discipline. Much of the literature on teacher training argued that improved teaching of writing would result from writing teachers' gaining theoretical knowledge. In other words, now that writing was considered (by some, at least) worthy of study, teacher trainers had a "content" they could ask new teachers to master. In its 1982 "Position Statement on the Preparation and Professional Development of Teachers of Writing," for instance, the CCCC task force insists that such teachers need both "experience in writing" and "theoretical knowledge to guide classroom practice" (446). In models such as this one, which emphasize theory and experience, theory was typically thought to *precede* practice—to be a body of knowledge to be translated and applied in classrooms. For instance, even as Richard Gebhardt argues for "balancing theory with practice" in teacher training, he suggests that teachers must *first* learn the "conceptual underpinnings" of the teaching of writing and then "test them out in practice" (1977, 134).

Likewise, just as the CCCC task force emphasizes the importance of acquiring knowledge in such areas as discourse theory, cognitive composing theory, and applied linguistics, Gebhardt's model for training writing teachers involves developing an expertise in the "structure and history of the English language" as well as acquiring a "solid understanding of rhetoric" (134). With Francis Christensen, whom he quotes, he agrees that new teachers should move through a sequence of courses beginning with grammar, moving to language history, and finally ending with composition. Drawing upon the NCTE book *What Every English Teacher Should Know,* Gebhardt suggests that the degree to which one has mastered rhetorical theory is directly related to one's ability to teach writing. A "good" teacher need only be able to recognize "such characteristics of good writing as substantial and relevant content; organization; clarity; appropriateness of tone," whereas a "superior" teacher should have a "detailed knowledge of theories and history of rhetoric" (Hook, Jacobs, and Crisp 1970, 135). Now that composition had a "body of knowledge," it could prepare teachers via the traditional model—scholarly acquisition.

The problem, I want to be clear, is not with the scholarship. Indeed, the growing research on the writing process enabled new possibilities for imagining both the epistemic act of writing and student writers, themselves. Rather, my concern is with how scholarship was thought to *function* in these teacher-training sites. Rather than scholarship and teaching working in an interdependent relationship to each other, the writing theory was positioned as the primary site of knowledge which, when translated, was thought to make for more thoughtful teaching practices. Following the research model, the transaction was one-way, with theory preceding and legitimizing teaching.

Perhaps most important, while changes in the university during the 1960s and 1970s—a growing student population, increased academic specialization, composition and rhetoric doctoral programs, and a body of process scholarship—resulted in both greater attention and new approaches to teacher training, one thing did not change: the institutional location of composition. As Sharon Crowley notes, "the introductory courses are still required, and composition teachers are still overworked and underpaid, just as they were prior to 1971" (1998, 213). What had changed was that the field now had a new group of composition professors, who were distinguished—because of their relationship to the discipline—from composition teachers. It was these professors who would produce composition scholarship, and who were often responsible for administering programs and preparing teachers of writing. That is, as a result of this new "specialty" in composition and rhetoric, English studies now had a group of experts, professors of writing pedagogy, who would take responsibility for the work no one else really wanted: preparing teachers of English. The pedagogical dimension of the field officially became, and has remained, composition's.

Compositionists as Change Agents: Writing Pedagogy into the Discipline

For better and for worse, composition has dutifully answered its charge to prepare future teachers, though often in less than ideal conditions. In fact, the conditions—typically occupying a space outside of the "official" curriculum, for instance, or compressed into a brief orientation or one-semester seminar—only make more visible the fortitude of the research-oriented discipline. And while compositionists have historically worked, and continue to work, in important ways to raise the status of teaching and to revise teacher-training practices, efforts that conform to the rules of the naturalized discipline are destined to be disciplined. One common "lesson" that can be gleaned from the historical examples I've cited above is that without change at the disciplinary level, it is difficult to move beyond familiar metaphors for preparing teachers: the teacher as scholar; the teacher as trainee or apprentice; the teacher as owner of his or her classroom and pedagogy.

As Latterell's 1996 study demonstrates, and my research confirms,[5] teacher-training programs (still) assume four major shapes: apprenticeships, practica, methods courses, and theory seminars. While orientations are common, thirty-two of the thirty-six responding institutions reported only a one-day orientation

(Latterell 1996, 10). The more extensive teaching practica or seminars tend to reify the familiar disciplinary distinction of teaching as a set of skills to be mastered—teacher as apprentice or trainee—or teaching as a body of knowledge to be mastered—teacher as scholar. In the former case, the practica are often tied directly to one's first semester of teaching, such that the curriculum is designed to help the new teacher adapt to a particular program (19). While this support is certainly important and necessary, the concern is that teacher training is a means to successful assimilation into a program, not a component of professorial development than one can study, reflect upon, and revise.

As composition studies continues to professionalize, theory courses become increasingly popular. In the Fall 1995 issue of *Composition Studies,* which features syllabi from seventeen graduate-level courses in composition, it is clear that graduate students are introduced to the field primarily by way of theory. Latterell's findings suggest that these seminars tend to serve as standalone courses, distinct from considerations of teaching practice (16). Often, in fact, the required course for TAs is the same as the gateway course for those graduate students intending to focus on composition and rhetoric. I agree with Leverenz and Goodburn that we need to attend to the differences between "how we might use published research and theory to prepare teachers new to composition and pedagogy to effectively teach undergraduates and how we use that work to introduce graduate students to the professionalized discourses of composition studies with which scholars are expected to be familiar" (23). While it makes good sense for teachers of first-year writing to engage the theoretical assumptions and values of the field, I worry not only that theory will take precedence over praxis, but also that we risk conflating an introduction to teaching first-year writing with an introduction to teaching English studies, whereby compositionists become "the only purveyors of pedagogical knowledge" (24). Of course, the absence of pedagogy courses elsewhere in the curriculum also suggests that graduate students' expertise in their subfield constitutes readiness to teach it.

All of these metaphors stem from a disciplinary structure in which there exists a deep and serious disjuncture between the *labor* of teaching and the *profession* of professing. In the first and last metaphors—teacher as scholar, teacher as owner—the status of teaching is presumably raised by mastery of scholarship or by the acquisition of private, individual space—both highly valued commodities in the corporate/academic economy. For instance, when TAs are allowed to teach courses outside of first-year writing, it is usually after having made significant scholarly progress (i.e., reaching upper-level coursework in literature). This teaching is not typically formally sponsored or supported, since it is presumably the coursework that prepares one for it. Advanced status grants the TA not only the right to teach in his or her subject area, but to be left alone in so doing.

The metaphors of teacher as apprentice or trainee position teaching as a craft or skill that can be learned by observing a master/manager. Though part-time instructors may never move beyond the class status of the apprentice, they become "token professionals" (Sosnoski 1994); on the other hand, TAs temporarily endure the system so that they can eventually assume the professional status of professor. In both cases, teaching remains something other than valued, intellectual, disciplinary work, and teachers are cast outside of disciplinary boundaries.

I agree with Slevin, then, that until the discipline is challenged, teaching will remain ancillary to research (even when the research is about pedagogy), and those of us interested in teaching will remain in a "permanently defensive position" (158). Responding defensively, we can only react to, and not alter, current structures. We need, then, to imagine ways to *act*—to alter not only the way we conceive of disciplinarity, but also the way we engage it. That is, we need to change both our minds and our behaviors. In many ways, Eble's discussion of the D.A. degree offers a compelling model for making pedagogy central to our disciplinary work. Of course, as I argue above, while the D.A. enabled the development of what might be the true definition of a teacher-scholar, it ultimately functioned to preserve the Ph.D. as a research degree, to maintain the professor as researcher. And yet, while D.A. programs were ultimately constrained by the research model—and dismantled when the need for college teachers diminished—the vision of the D.A. has not disappeared.

Graduates from these programs continue to promote pedagogy-centered visions through scholarship and programs across the country. To point to one well-documented example, the D.A. program at SUNY–Albany, which put issues of writing theory and practice, critical theory, and literary studies in dialogue with teaching theory and practice, eventually became—at least for a while—an innovative and pedagogy-centered doctoral program (see North 2000 and Berlin 1996 for discussions of this program). This innovative work, however modest, reminds us that small steps can be taken on the local level, in ways that put important pressure on the discipline, changing the way it is enacted.

Those of us in composition can and do occupy a similar role—working to promote pedagogy-centered visions from the disciplinary margins. As Crowley notes, academics who profess composition studies go about their work differently than many of their colleagues in literature:

> [Composition's] interest in pedagogy inverts the traditional academic privileging of theory over practice and research over teaching. Composition scholarship typically focuses on the process of learning rather than on the acquisition of knowledge, and composition pedagogy focuses on change and development in students rather than on transmission of a heritage. (1998, 3)

Because of this approach, Slevin argues, "composition, as a discipline, should endeavor to gain and exercise 'academic leadership,' [or, more accurately, pedagogical leadership] by which I mean the ability (specifically, the authority and the power) to change institutions so that they do a better job of educating students" (1996, 153).

Of course, now that composition itself has gained disciplinary status, it can (and does) promote this new vision in its growing number of graduate programs and seminars. But I would argue that our greatest opportunity to instigate disciplinary and pedagogical change comes, ironically, in the location that exists outside of traditional disciplinary boundaries: teacher-preparation sites. Because compositionists are uniquely positioned to shape the people who will become (and teach) the next generation of English professors, we can work to teach doctoral students a new way of enacting pedagogy, and of professing English. That is to say, we can use our location not only to change the way we prepare teachers, but also to help exert pressure on how we introduce the next generation to the disciplinary practices and behaviors of English studies. Changing the way we teach doctoral students to understand, enact, and value pedagogy is a crucial step to changing the way they carry out their disciplinary work.

In many ways, I am advocating at the level of teacher training what Susan Miller argued, more than a decade ago, for first-year writing: that we see our work with new teachers as a "culturally designated place for political [and disciplinary] action" (1991, 186). As she writes, "Composition studies has always had the process available to transform its marginalized culture into a site where cultural superstructures and their privileging results are visibly put into question. An actually improved status depends on openly consolidating the field's internal, existing resistances to the cultural superstructure that first defined it" (186). Likewise, through our teaching of pedagogy, we can help new teachers not only examine and critique disciplinary structures and the entrenched notions of professing that result, but also take steps toward changing the way they enact the discipline. Of course, the "trick," as Murphy notes, is "to find ways to capitalize on the unique pedagogical institutional forum proved by the service expectation without being co-opted either politically or intellectually by the educational and cultural agendas seeking to define the nature of the service being provided" (2000, 31).

If we remain the primary purveyors of pedagogy in our discipline, however, I believe the chances of being co-opted are great. While educating the next generation of English studies differently means teaching those in all subfields (not just composition) a different conception of disciplinarity, we can also enact this revisionary work by inviting our colleagues from all areas of English studies to participate in opportunities for ongoing teacher development. Indeed, to make departmental changes like those I described in the introduction to this chapter, engaging issues of pedagogy with our colleagues becomes crucial. I address issues of ongoing development specifically in Chapter 5.

The kind of change I am advocating is not quick or easy. It is not about abiding by the familiar process whereby change is instigated from the top down; a new vision is created by scholars, which is meant to alter practices at the ground level. Instead, it is about returning to our praxis-oriented, pragmatic roots in composition, remembering, as Stanley Fish contends, "pragmatism is the philosophy not of grand ambitions but of little steps" (1998, 432). It also means changing the pedagogy of our field, which is becoming increasingly disciplined, as we have traded our emphasis on praxis for a body of knowledge. As North articulated more than a decade ago: "The school subject, composition, consisted almost entirely of knowledge produced by Practitioner inquiry [. . .]. And what marks [composition and rhetoric's] emergence as a nascent academic field more than anything else is this need to replace practice as the field's dominant mode of inquiry" (1987, 15).

If composition is to take a leadership role in educating the next generation of English professors differently, then the field will have to examine its complicity in disciplinary (and corporate) structures. As Peter Vandenberg notes, "The short history of composition studies has been one of appropriation—appropriation of the same disciplinary categories and attitudes that seemed oppressive when used to characterize literary studies. [. . .] In doing so, it has stumbled into the academy's disciplinary memory, reconstructing a class-based system of inequality in (re)claimed institutional space" (1998, 23). (See also Ferry 1998; Trimbur 1996; Crowley 1998). It will need, that is, to return to its roots of practitioner-based inquiry so as to change the discipline from the bottom up, by promoting a new conception of pedagogy as well as new pedagogy-centered disciplinary practices.

This means taking a careful look at our most recent move to make pedagogy a new disciplinary subject. As I argue above, I am concerned that changing the "subject" to pedagogy is not enough; changing the knowledge body does not result in new disciplinary behaviors or values. The establishment of an expert class of pedagogy specialists may offer us academic legitimacy within the current model, but it does little to change the status of teaching in the discipline, to alter the way we conceive of the professor in the first place. In the next chapter, I will begin where I leave off here, with the metaphor that has held most prevalent over time, and which, I will argue, continues to inform both composition's rise to disciplinarity and the current "pedagogical boom" in English studies: the teacher as scholar.

The Teacher as Scholar

No metaphor has played a greater role in the professorial
enterprise than that of "teacher as scholar." In the traditional professorial model, teaching is positioned as the by-product of research, and teacher development is thought to "naturally" follow scholarly development. We take for granted that
the dissertation is the culminating experience of the doctoral process, and that the ability to produce scholarship sanctions one to
profess it to others. We rarely question the fact that students'
scholarly progress is nurtured and publicly supported through
seminars, publishing workshops, and close mentoring from their
dissertation chairs, while support for teaching development occurs much less officially, often in spaces marginal to the doctoral
curriculum.

With the recent "turn" to the pedagogical in English studies,
we see efforts to rewrite this metaphor, to claim teaching as intellectual work in its own right and to rewrite the subject position
of teacher as a professional intellectual. Henry Giroux and Peter
McLaren, whose critical pedagogy discourse has gained increasing currency in the discipline, argue for the teacher as "transformative intellectual," one "who exercises forms of intellectual and
pedagogical practice which attempt to insert teaching and learning directly into the political sphere" (1986, 215).

For those in composition, who have long centered our work
on teaching and learning, many would say this pedagogical turn
and new articulation of the teacher is good news; it has allowed
the field to achieve a status it could not accomplish on its own.
As Worsham puts its, "pedagogy has become not only a legitimate object of intellectual inquiry in English studies, a boom subject in the humanities, but also a matter of urgent social and
political interest" (1998, 217). But her concern, and my own, is
that in our eagerness to transform our field from the status of

"nobodiness" to "somebodiness," we have maintained a rather uncritical relationship to critical pedagogy; it is this relationship I will explore here. In what ways has critical pedagogy scholarship helped us to rethink the relationship between teaching and professing?

But it is not only critical pedagogy discourse that has helped make the phrase "teacher as scholar" more familiar in our academic institutions. Ernest Boyer's 1990 *Scholarship Reconsidered,* in which he seeks to move us beyond the age-old dichotomy of teaching versus research, initiated a surge of interest in the "scholarship of teaching." As this movement takes hold in our universities, it is worth exploring the model of the "teacher as scholar" it promotes, the conception of pedagogy it forwards, and the way each works in dialogue (or dissonance) with the teacher research composition has long promoted. As with the critical pedagogy movement, composition gains credibility because of a pedagogy movement from the outside; what is gained and lost, as a result?

In this chapter, I will consider the teacher as scholar articulated in both the critical pedagogy and scholarship-of-teaching movements, examining the extent to which they depart from— or maintain—traditional disciplinary practices. I then move on to offer an alternative model of reflexive[1] pedagogical inquiry, on which I will build throughout the book.

Composition Meets Critical Pedagogy

For those of us in composition, it might be easy to deny that a model privileging the scholar over the teacher, and separating their work, plays a determining role in our professional activities. After all, we might contend, our field is built around interactions with students. Our scholarship is often, explicitly or implicitly, tied to the classroom. We cannot do our research without considering its pedagogical implications. As Christine Farris and Chris Anson argue in the introduction to their 1998 collection, we have been "reluctant to assume a top-down, research-to-theory-to-practice relationship" and instead favor a "dialectical relationship between theory and practice" (3). We promote teacher-scholars, not teachers *as* scholars.

Whether these claims are borne out in practice is debatable. But what is certain is that composition has been institutionally and intellectually devalued for such principles. And for this reason, it makes sense that composition has linked itself with critical pedagogy. This is not to suggest that this alliance is entirely driven by self-promotion; after all, the fields share (or claim to share) many of the same foundations: a belief in pedagogy as intellectual inquiry, a valuing of student knowledge, and a hope that pedagogy will act as a catalyst for personal, or even cultural, change. Perhaps most important, both fields claim to be centered on engagement among people, rather than the transmission of knowledge. As Giroux writes,

> [Pedagogy] becomes an act of cultural production, a form of "writing" in which the process by which power is inscribed on the body and implicated in the production of desire, knowledge, and values begins not with a particular claim to postdisciplinary knowledge but with real people articulating and rewriting their lived experiences within, rather than outside, history. (1995, 8)

But it is not this engagement with people that has allowed composition disciplinary credibility. Indeed, composition has not gained "middle class status" (Trimbur) by emphasizing those characteristics that make it *unlike* traditional disciplines; rather, it has "boomed" by demonstrating that it has what it takes to fit in with its disciplinary siblings: a growing body of scholarly research and publications, graduate programs, national conferences, journals, and book series. Perhaps most important, composition has demonstrated its willingness to abide by a particular mode of subject formation in service of professionalism. As John Trimbur argues, professionalism "is all about the cultural authorization of expertise":

> [P]rofessionals and academics learn to recognize themselves and to enact identities as the subjects of disciplined discourses and practices precisely to the extent that they assume the rhetorical authority to speak as experts, in an asymmetrical relationship,

on behalf of a client populations of laypersons who need or want
their services. (1996, 138)

That is to say, part of what it means to become a composition professional involves setting oneself apart from those who
are not a part of that group, those who are excluded from the
disciplinary boundaries. Christopher Ferry puts it simply: "We
are talking, finally, about a gap between a knowledge-making
'professional' class and a teaching working class" (1998, 14).

The professional (publishing) compositionist, then, has gained
disciplinary legitimacy not because teaching has become a valued practice, but because the teacher has been remade in the
scholar's image. In much the same way, critical pedagogues are
bearers of "critical knowledge, rules, and values through which
they consciously articulate and problematize their relationship
to each other, to students, to subject matter, and to the wider
community" (Giroux and McLaren 1986, 225). As Ira Shor has
it, "[T]he dialogical teacher is more intellectually developed, more
practiced in critical scrutiny, and more committed to a political
dream of social change than are the students" (1980, 95). Or, I
might add, than are his or her *un*critical teaching colleagues.

Consequently, the answer to the question, "How does one
become a critical teacher?" seems to be fairly consistent: "by learning the tradition of critical pedagogy." The implication is that
the enactment of the pedagogy—the specific strategies by which
it is engaged with students—is secondary and subordinate to the
acquisition of the scholarship. It follows, then, that those who
compose the scholarship on pedagogy are privileged above those
who teach. In fact, in mainstream critical pedagogy discourse,
the scholar often serves as the idealized subject, the being to which
teachers should aspire.

Becoming the Critical Teacher

Drawing from Michel Foucault, Gore (1993) argues that since
all pedagogies promote an ideal subject, we must examine in pedagogical discourses not only how this ideal subject is constructed,

but how one becomes this subject—what is "disciplined," "styled," or altered in the name of this ideal.

In critical pedagogy discourse, the ideal subject is the teacher as "critical" or "transformative" intellectual. Giroux and McLaren describe him or her as

> one who exercises forms of intellectual and pedagogical practice, which attempt to insert teaching and learning directly into the political sphere by arguing that schooling represents both a struggle for meaning and a struggle over power relations. [. . .] Teachers who assume the role of transformative intellectual treat students as critical agents, question how knowledge is produced and distributed, utilize dialogue, and make knowledge meaningful, critical, and ultimately emancipatory. (215)

But what does it mean to educate teachers as transformative intellectuals? In their article "Teacher Education and the Politics of Engagement," Giroux and McLaren contend that teacher-education programs too often define teachers as technicians. Rather than fostering in teachers a "critical understanding," so that they may, in turn, help promote the development of students as active, critical citizens, these programs tend to emphasize "standardization, competency, and narrowly-defined performance skills" (1986, 219). Kenneth Zeichner weighs in with the hope that future debate within teacher education "will be more concerned with the question of which educational, moral and political commitments ought to guide our work in the field rather than with the practice of merely dwelling on which procedures and organizations will most effectively help us realize tacit and often unexamined ends" (1983, 8).

While the ends and goals are certainly clear enough in critical pedagogy scholarship, there is little time granted to the "procedure and organizations" that will help promote a critical pedagogy, or the development of critical teachers. In fact, critical pedagogy discourses go so far to challenge the conflation of good teaching with "technical expertise" that they often inadvertently position teaching *practices* as necessarily instrumental, mechanistic. More important than developing critical pedagogical processes, this scholarship teaches, is the acquisition of critical *knowledge.*

In fact, in promoting a new brand of teacher education, Giroux and McLaren claim they must "forego a detailed specification of teaching practices" (228); they do, however, offer a sketch of the kind of teacher they seek to promote, as well as the type of critical knowledge they believe teachers must acquire. Not surprisingly, the two are necessarily intertwined. One becomes an emancipatory authority *because* he or she bears "critical knowledge." This brings us right back, of course, to a traditional notion of the relationship between research and teaching, whereby one's teaching is improved as a result of access to and mastery of a particular content.

Indeed, Giroux and McLaren contend that teacher-education programs must provide teachers with the "critical terminology and conceptual apparatus that will allow them not only to critically analyze the democratic and political shortcomings of schools, but also to develop the knowledge and skills that will advance the possibilities for generating curricula, classroom social practices, and organizational arrangements based on and cultivating a deep respect for a democratic and ethically-based community" (223). On many levels, their work is crucial. It insists that what-works practices should not be substituted for rich understandings of pedagogy as necessarily theoretical, historical, and social. But if we forgo a discussion of practice altogether, instructional acts too easily become the natural by-product of critical knowledge, left for teachers to unpack and engage.

Training Critical Teachers in Composition

Because it is the acquisition of the "critical tradition" that is thought to stand in for "training," there are relatively few examples of specific instructional acts designed to promote "critical" teacher development in first-year writing programs. But in the examples of teacher-training scholarship I have found that work out of the "critical movement," we see tendencies to position knowledge and tradition as precursors to teaching. In Nancy Welch's "Resisting the Faith: Conversion, Resistance, and the Training of Teachers," she narrates her experience in two teacher-training programs, one of which is based on critical cultural theories. The teaching seminar consisted of weekly meetings with a group of "established" teachers, and was designed to "guide new teachers into speaking a particular language and accepting a particular set of assumptions about teaching and the world" (1993, 394). This process was fueled largely by engaging the "right" scholarship; for instance, students read Foucault's "What Is an Author?" and then were asked to compose a paper describing a "Foucauldian classroom." Practice, in this case, was thought to follow theory. Additionally, new teachers were asked to visit the classrooms of "established teachers"—presumably already fluent in the correct language and scholarly knowledge required by the program. Welch describes taking "copious notes" on the "ideal teacher" she observed, so as to work toward disciplining herself into the model.

In this context new teachers were regarded not only as lacking legitimate pedagogical visions of their own, but as working out of a state of false consciousness that could be cured by the proper scholarly inoculation. While this example is admittedly an extreme one, the assumption remains that it is critical knowledge—passed down from someone who makes it, or has privileged access to it—that prepares one to teach.

Tori Haring-Smith's "The Importance of Theory in the Training of Teaching Assistants" offers an example of what Wendy Bishop calls the "competing theories" approach. Here, teachers are offered a survey of competing theories, the assumption being that "[n]o teacher of composition, indeed, no teacher of any subject, can operate without some kind of conscious or unconscious theory. No action we take is neutral in that respect" (1985, 35). For Haring-Smith teachers are already working out of theoretical positions—in fact, she insists that teachers be positioned as "thinkers," not "clones or apprentices" (36). What teachers need, then, is assistance in making those positions visible and examining them. She thus advocates a pedagogy that enables teachers to study a range of theoretical frameworks that might inform their own practices, so that they may "engage in self-reflection and self-evaluation" (35).

For Haring-Smith, then, teaching is not the by-product of theory, but is itself an epistemic practice. Even so, her language illuminates how deeply ingrained is the distinction between theory and practice—how difficult it is to move away from separating the two. She writes, "The ideal training program for TAs combines a healthy *dose* of theory with a *translation* of that theory into practice" (35; my emphasis). Here her language might be read to suggest that theory is a deliverable content of which teachers are in need, and which, upon receipt, is then translated into practice. If this is the case, then teachers do not play a role in developing the theory; it is presumably created outside of the classroom and delivered to them. The particular example Haring-Smith provides asks students to read a set of theories and then to generate assignments or exercises that grow out of it. "Every week students must come prepared not only to discus the intrinsic merits and effects of given theories but also to demonstrate how those theories can be put into practice in a composition classroom" (35).

While I, like Haring-Smith, work to offer my students a range of pedagogical perspectives and theories, I worry about the potential of such "competing theories" methods to reify the traditional assumption that it is scholarly knowledge that prepares one to teach, and that there exists a one-way dynamic between scholarship and teaching. Indeed, I am interested in the ways that students' practices as teachers *speak back* to the theories they engage, the ways those practices make meaning and are themselves theoretical.

While I don't want to downplay the importance of regarding pedagogy as an intellectual site of inquiry, my concern is that merely changing the subject to pedagogy does not mean we have moved beyond the traditional disciplinary model whereby one "class" (of scholars) makes the knowledge and another (of teachers) enacts it. While the teacher is encouraged to master the pedagogy scholarship he or she wants to enact in the room, he or she is not invited to contribute to it, to participate in its making. As Chris Gallagher argues, critical pedagogy functions as a "theoretical tradition upon which teachers may draw, but to which they may not contribute" (2000, 76). I am worried, then, not only that this new body of pedagogy scholarship reinforces the notion that scholarship prepares one to teach, but that it only strengthens the divide between (pedagogical) researchers and teachers.

This does not mean scholars have nothing to say to teachers, or that teachers won't benefit from engaging pedagogy scholarship. My concern, though, is with what is lost when pedagogical visions are valued above pedagogical practices. With Ruth Ray I concur that many reform efforts in education occur from the "bottom up," through the "questioning and experimenting of teachers attempting to solve real problems in their classrooms" (1993, 71). And, in fact, if teachers position themselves as classroom researchers, she argues, they will be better able to critically engage theory, to respond to and contribute to it. This leads me to another movement connected to the teacher-as-scholar metaphor, one that seeks to position the teacher as a researcher in his or her own classroom.

The Scholarship of Teaching

Thus far, I have used "scholar" to signify a magisterial figure, one who stands above his or her readers, offering prescriptive visions to those below. In the last decade, however, we've witnessed a growing cross-disciplinary movement called "the scholarship of teaching" that argues for the teacher as a researcher in his or her own classroom, and promotes a disciplined study of pedagogical *practice*. While Ernest Boyer is often credited for spearheading this movement, the institutional realities that provided the context for his words certainly aided his argument. For instance, as the 2000 *MLA Newsletter* article "Job Market Remains Competitive" makes clear, the combination of an overproduction of Ph.D.s and a shortage of tenure-track positions means that two-thirds of job candidates find themselves employed by institutions very different from the research universities where they did graduate work. Despite heavy teaching loads and lip service offered by colleges to the triad of teaching, research, and service, the relative weight granted to teaching is rarely equivalent to the realities of the job (Boyer). According to the Carnegie Foundation's 1989 National Survey of Faculty, which Boyer cites, the requirements of rank and tenure at most four-year institutions continue to place most emphasis on refereed research articles. As Boyer notes, "Good teaching is expected, but is often inadequately assessed" (28). Richard I. Miller's 1990 survey of academic vice presidents and deans at more than eight hundred colleges and universities further demonstrates the imbalance of value given to teaching versus research (Boyer 29). Only 5 percent observed a shift toward teaching in recent years; in fact, at doctoral institutions, 56 percent noted a move toward research and away from teaching and service.

By 1994, when the Carnegie Foundation conducted a follow-up national survey of 1,380 four-year colleges and universities with a 63 percent response rate, the situation looked better. The survey offers evidence that efforts to redefine faculty roles are underway: at least three-quarters of respondents said they had already made changes to reward good teaching, such as giving awards for teaching excellence or offering incentives for professors to improve their teaching. Additionally, we see new national efforts including the Carnegie Academy for the Scholarship of Teaching and Learning and the American Association for Higher Education Peer Review Project, designed to challenge faculty-reward systems and promote teaching as a scholarly enterprise. Still, Charles Glassick, Mary Taylor Huber, and Gene Maeroff reported in *Scholarship Assessed: Evaluation of the Professoriate* (1997) that only 50 percent of the country's colleges and universities offered merit raises to reward good teaching, and only 28 percent had established centers for improving teaching on their campuses (17). Moreover, as they argue, evaluation tends to remain "obsessed with numbers," shortchanging teaching and service work which can't easily be quantified. They cite the 1994 Carnegie survey, in which over 70 percent of American professors contend that "better ways to evaluate teaching performance" are needed at their universities (20).

Of course, as Gebhardt (1997) reminds us, efforts to articulate teaching as scholarly work were underway long before Boyer's 1990 publication, and by now include those of the National Endowments for the Humanities, the National Council of Teachers of English, the Modern Language Association, the Institutional Priorities and Faculty Awards Project and the AAUP (Minter and Goodburn 2002). In fact, the growing use of the term "scholarship of teaching" (as if it were new) might well result in perplexity on the part of compositionists: "What's new about this? We've been doing this forever!" True enough: as Deborah Minter and Amy Goodburn point out in the introduction to their 2002 collection, composition has long worked to promote similar goals to those of the scholarship-of-teaching movement. Most notably, the field has produced much scholarship on the uses of portfolios as a holistic and developmental means of assessment (as in the work of such scholars as Robert Yagelski, Wendy Bishop, Chris Anson, Karen Black, Liz Hamp-Lyons, Peter Elbow, and Amy Goodburn), and has espoused and enacted a strong commitment to "teacher research," scholarship that illuminates how "scenes of learning and teaching within writing classrooms can be documented in ways that expand and deepen our understanding of literacy learning as well as particular pedagogical approaches" (Minter and Goodburn 2002, xvii; see also Ray 1993; Fleischer 2000;, Lee 2000; Welch 1997; Gallagher 2002; Boquet 2002; Qualley 1997).

As with the critical pedagogy movement, momentum from the outside has proved necessary for teacher-research work to be deemed viable and legitimate, to be embraced by scholars outside of the fields of English and education. As Minter and Goodburn point out, it is somewhat disconcerting to see how distinct the scholarship-of-teaching movement remains from teacher research in composition (xvii). But perhaps we should not be surprised, since many organized efforts to improve the status of teaching are located outside of disciplines and departments (e.g., Preparing Future Faculty and the Consortium on the Preparation of Graduate Students as College Teachers, or even the growing number of centers for excellence in teaching and learning). Publications like the *Journal of Scholarship of Teaching and Learning* publish work from scholars of all disciplines, requiring them to abide by one of several available research methodologies (more on this later), and by the premise that good teaching practices and processes reach across disciplinary and institutional contexts.

The rationale for this requirement is partly to help teachers document their work so that those in other fields can understand it, particularly those who assess teaching for purposes such as tenure and promotion. And certainly cross-disciplinary conversations are exciting and important.[2] My concern, however, is that

an overreliance on methodology or templates may result in a flat-
tening out of crucial contexts and questions that enable development and inquiry. Indeed, in her study of pedagogy journals across
disciplines, Maryellen Weimer points out that an emphasis on
"technique" too often results in a lack of attention to rationale
and context (1993, 45–46). As important as it is to refrain from
privileging pedagogical theories over practices (as does critical
pedagogy discourse), it is also important that we not simply overturn the theory/practice binary and privilege practice in isolation
from the theories that animate it. More specifically, my appre-
hension is that teaching is granted scholarly value because it can
be "fit" into a predetermined scholarly approach, not because
pedagogy, itself, has been reconceived as an important mode of
knowledge production.

Composing the Scholarship of Teaching

If the critical pedagogue is a "master" of critical knowledge, then
the teacher-scholar (as defined by the Carnegie Foundation) is a
scientific researcher in his or her classroom. Teacher research is
certainly a practice I advocate, as it has been defined in composition (Ray 1993; Fleischer 2000; Lee 2000). This new conception
of the teacher as researcher, however, needs some unpacking.

A look at the editorial process of the *Journal of Scholarship
of Teaching and Learning* (*JoSoTL*) helps illustrate the ideal subject being promoted. While the editors concede that there are no
"agreed-upon" criteria for what counts as teaching scholarship,
they abide by the conception promoted by Lee Shulman, the presi-
dent of the Carnegie Foundation:

> For an activity to be designated as scholarship, it should mani-
> fest at least three key characteristics: It should be public, suscep-
> tible to critical review and evaluation, and accessible for exchange
> and use by other members of one's scholarly community. We
> thus observe, with respect to all forms of scholarship, that they
> are acts of mind or spirit that have been made public in some
> manner, have been subjected to peer review by members of one's
> intellectual or professional community, and can be cited, refuted,
> built upon, and shared among members of that community. Schol-

arship properly communicated and critiqued serves as the build-ing blocks for knowledge growth in a field. ("Course Anatomy," para. 3)

The editors then draw from *Scholarship Assessed* (Glassick, Huber, and Maeroff 1997), to outline six qualitative standards they promote in evaluating the submission to *JoSoTL*:

♦ Clear Goals. What is the purpose of the scholarship and are the goals clearly stated?

♦ Adequate Preparation. Does the scholar have the prerequisite skills to thoroughly investigate the problem?

♦ Appropriate Methods. Scholarship must be carried out compe-tently for the results to have credibility. Did the scholar use the appropriate procedures to investigate the problem?

♦ Significant Results. Does the scholarship help build the knowl-edge base in the field?

♦ Effective Presentation. Does the scholarship meet the standards or quality for the medium in which it is presented?

♦ Reflective Critique. Is there evidence that the scholar has learned from the experience and can apply this knowledge to future prob-lems?

As these criteria suggest, the scholarship of teaching tends to promote a problem-solving model, whereby teaching is presented as a linear process that begins with a question and ends with a result that can be applied to future classroom work. (The as-sumption, of course, is that teaching problems or questions *have* definite solutions.)

One widely used methodology is classroom action research.[3] In the second volume of *JoSoTL*, Gwynn Mettetal offers a "how to" for conducting such research, a method which she locates in the middle of a continuum that ranges from "personal reflec-tion" on one end to "formal empirical studies" on the other (2001, 7). (Personal reflection, however, is not commonly found in schol-arship on teaching, as it does not lend itself to the above assess-ment criteria). The process of classroom action research is based on a model that involves identifying a question or problem, re-viewing current literature, planning a research strategy (which should include data of some kind), gathering data, making sense of data, taking action, and sharing one's findings (9).

Indeed, there are many pedagogical projects served by this methodology. For instance, Nancy Hunt's "Does Mid-Semester Feedback Make a Difference?" (2003) offers "institution-specific 'proof'" that midsemester feedback results in a positive experience for students and teachers alike. Presenting "proof" (which comes here from student and teacher survey responses) was crucial to Hunt's project since, in her program, faculty were "reluctant" to take on additional assessment without evidence that it would make a difference. Her article provides not only this evidence, but also sample questions to aid teachers in developing feedback tools. Because this practice does require more work on the teacher's part, the inclusion of these examples—which might serve as a starting point for teachers across disciplines—is important.

In "A Model for Student Success: Critical Thinking and 'At Risk' Students," psychology professor Randall E. Osborne seeks to challenge the notion that critical thinking cannot be taught, and suggests a model for critical thinking pedagogy that "can be employed regardless of one's discipline" (2000, abstract). He argues that there is often a discrepancy between faculty expectations for students' preparation and students' own perceptions of their abilities. Many students note, for instance, that critical thinking is not only "under-appreciated" in high school, but also often punished (42). Osborne goes on to describe a pilot program at his university in which an introductory psychology course was paired with a course on critical thinking, and concludes with data to suggest that the GPAs of students in the paired course (overall and in psychology) were higher than those of their peers outside the study. Again, this quantitative evidence is likely compulsory to prove to administrators (and by extension to the scholarship-of-teaching audience) that such a course is necessary and that it will result in improved grades and perhaps even better student retention.

However, as Beth Daniell points out, those of us who work in the humanities (and even social sciences) often find that our theories do not do a good job of predicting, of offering measurable or replicable results. Students, certainly, have a way of "defying prediction" (1994, 129), and in writing classes where student texts occupy the center of the class pedagogies have to be worked out every time anew. So rather than abiding by a predictive model —whereby a practice or theory is thought to produce positive results—teacher-scholars in fields like composition more often rely on interpretive approaches, which tend to be "incommensurate rather than comprehensive" (129). Interpretive approaches position theory not as "above belief but in front of it" (130), foregrounding the notion that our lenses are always political, serve the interests of some group or discipline, and promote particular beliefs and assumptions. Here the beliefs, assumptions, and values we bring to the classroom—and the ways they are negotiated in particular classrooms with students—are as important to examine as are the "results" of our pedagogies, which are likely to be different with every pedagogical encounter.

We might consider, then, what is lost by the approaches described above. What does it mean, for instance, to measure student success by GPA? While Osborne sets out to prove that critical thinking can be taught (using the cognitive levels of Bloom's taxonomy), his methodology doesn't allow the teacher to consider the kinds of critical thinking students already bring to the classroom. Nor does it enable us to consider the dialogic process of engaging in critical thinking with particular students in specific institutional contexts. While Osborne's project is necessarily a political one—he seeks to aid the entry of "at-risk" students into the academy—his values, beliefs, and assumptions remain implicit, unaddressed. These issues may not lie within the scope of Osborne's essay, and may not help him to prove to others that critical thinking must and can be taught. Nevertheless, I worry that the scholarship of teaching may emphasize outcomes at the expense of attention to the development and growth of teachers in specific pedagogical situations.

This is not to say that scholarship of teaching does not include such work. Melinda Swensen's "Preparing Teachers and Students for Narrative Learning," while classified as classroom action research, works against the grain of prevailing discourse practices by emphasizing process more than results and accounting for the difficulties and tensions teachers experience as they move from a more comfortable teacher-centered approach to a more risky student-centered one. She highlights the ways teachers must change: they must assess which aspects of their teaching aren't working, examine which philosophies inform their pedagogies, and consider how they were taught as students (2001, 5). Swensen also offers a set of questions to make one's teaching "unfamiliar" and thus open to inquiry, promotes "constant self-critique and re-commitment to changing" and offers methods to promote improved teacher inquiry (7, 9). At the same time, she emphasizes that her methods are specific to the group with whom she works—they are not simply transferable. While Swensen's piece offers no quantitative evidence or proof that the practice-based learning approach she advocates is the best approach, she offers a thorough discussion of the theories that inform this vision as well as concrete ways to examine one's own pedagogical goals and practices. Her piece, which does seem to be an exception, helps others engage in the scholarship of teaching.

While the scholarship of teaching offers many possibilities for institutional change, my concern is that the crucial issues raised by poststructuralist thought—the importance of context, the partiality of knowledge, the multiplicity and fluidity of subjects, the power dynamics at work in every pedagogical situation—are not easily addressed within the methodologies promoted. As Daniell argues, we need also to ask:

> How valid and how rigorous is the research that supports this theory? What phenomena does this theory fail to take into account? That is, where does it "leak"? Can we state the limitations of theory, so that we do not claim more for it than it can do, so that we can caution others that this theory works in this domain but not in that one? What are the assumptions, both stated and unstated, on which that theory rests? (131)

While the discussion of "leaks" in theories, practices, and methodologies may seem to point to deficits or flaws, I would rather approach them as possibilities. What is flattened out or repressed within this model? What have I not accounted for? Who has not been heard? In these "leaks" may lie opportunities for reflection and resistance, and for consideration of what educational structures and methods of representation require us to repress (Ellsworth 1989; Orner 1992; Miller 1991). I want to be clear, however, that this is not an argument against attention to methodology; instead, I am concerned that we not privilege a search for "one true" methodology over an ongoing inquiry into our teaching.

Training the Teacher-Researcher

As I've suggested above, how we define "teacher-researcher" largely informs the way in which we seek to prepare teacher-scholars. The teacher-scholar promoted by the Carnegie movement, and the teacher research that results, for instance, would likely require a different development/training process than would the teacher-scholar promoted in composition (see Ray 1993; Fleischer 2000; Lee 2000; Qualley 1997; Welch 1997; Boquet 2002). Linda Brodkey's distinction between "analytic" and "interpretive" ethnography is useful here. Analytic approaches to teacher research (or any kind of research), like predictive methods, are largely product-oriented; they are most interested in discovering certainties and reporting found truths. Interpretive approaches, on the other hand, are driven by doubt and uncertainty; they are process-oriented and context-specific, and approach knowledge as necessarily constructed socially and rhetorically (qtd. in Ray 1993, 141).

Teacher research that stems from the scholarship-on-teaching movement tends to be informed by the analytical model. This means that teachers learning to engage these methods need to learn, first and foremost, a methodology for studying their classrooms and reporting the resulting data. In many ways, this approach represents the other side of the coin relied on by the critical pedagogy movement; instead of mastering a new body of pedagogy knowledge, teachers must master an approach to analyzing their teaching. They must also learn methods of creating measurable objectives for assignments and units and for incorporating a range of pedagogical methods designed to reach different types of learners. Of course, there are good reasons for this approach, particularly since one aim of this movement is to demonstrate that teaching can be analyzed and assessed in the same ways research can. The movement functions, in fact, to demonstrate how the scholarship of teaching can fit into an already-existing disciplinary model.[4]

As Mary Taylor Huber points out, however, this need not be the case. In fact, she argues, "if scholarly attention to teaching and learning in higher education is to gain through multi- or interdisciplinary exchange, then a variety of questions need to be asked and a variety of approaches should flourish. [. . .] The challenge here is to reconceptualize relationships between the disciplines, so that the lessons flow in all directions rather than demanding the diffusion of one privileged way of knowing" (2000, 9).

In Goodburn's "(Re)Viewing Teaching as Intellectual Work in English Studies," for instance, she describes the limits and possibilities of representing one's teaching as a text for external reviews to assess. The six reviews she received made her aware of "how assessments of my performance as a teacher were intimately tied to my performance as a portfolio author" (2002, 92), which in turn led her to consider what can and cannot be represented within the portfolio genre. While Goodburn makes clear that the peer reviews did serve her—they helped her to think more deeply about assessment for student learning, about how the (oft-taken-for-granted) institutional contexts in which she teaches shape her pedagogical visions and values, and about how her course fits in relation to similar courses across the country—she also argues that we need to consider both "new ways of reading our teaching" and "new communities of readers who are qualified to assess and evaluate such representations" (101).

Indeed, this is where Minter and Goodburn's contention that there needs to be greater cross-conversation between the scholarship-of-teaching movement and composition studies comes in. As they ask in their introduction, "How does our understanding of textuality inform our representations of the classroom? How do theories of collaboration inform the construction of teaching portfolios, which are conceived in primarily individualistic terms? What do our theories of reading mean for how we read our representations of teaching?" (2002, xvii). And I would add other questions: How do our understandings of development (Haswell 1991) and revision inform our conception of teacher research?

How do poststructuralist theories of subjectivity affect our representation of the teaching self? How do we take into account the rhetorical context of our meaning making? How do we, as David Bartholomae promotes, place adequate value on the important learning that accompanies "undoing," disrupting, or confusing (1996, 14) instead of on mastery and acquisition (both for those who compose teacher research as well as those who read it)?

The Pedagogy of Our Arguments

We learn from the above examples that it takes more than scholarship *on* pedagogy to alter the relationship between teaching and research, between teachers and researchers. Critical education scholarship that "promotes" pedagogy to the level of abstraction—knowledge to be mastered more than engaged—in fact only replicates the most traditional professorial model. At the same time, we also need to look with a critical eye at scholarship that values methodology over an epistemic process of inquiry, or requires us to leave out moments and questions that might greatly enable development. This is certainly not to say that scholarship on pedagogy does not serve teachers and scholars; rather, I believe that we need to attend more carefully to what Gore calls the "pedagogy of our arguments," the choices we make in writing about teaching (as many of us in composition do), as well as the ways we engage, and teach students to engage, this scholarship. We need, that is, to conceptualize and compose pedagogy scholarship differently; we need to make pedagogy scholarship more *praxis-oriented*.

I draw from Paulo Freire's now-familiar term, praxis, to highlight those characteristics that distinguish this pedagogical inquiry from pedagogy scholarship that abides by the traditional disciplinary model. First, praxis-oriented scholarship emphasizes dialogue between action and reflection; neither one, in itself, is sufficient. Scholarship that offers *only* visions or *only* methods, without an examination of how theory and practice function dialectically, does not go far enough. Second, praxis is a human endeavor, and thus involves a dialogue among humans: teachers, scholars, and students. Enacting praxis means refusing a top-down model, whereby theory can be given to those who are seemingly "lacking" it. Instead, theory must be made, through dialogue, by its participants. Praxis refuses the very notion of a magister, because, as Freire reminds us, dialogue cannot exist without humility. "How can I dialogue if I always project ignorance onto others and never perceive my own?" he asks (1993, 71). In praxis-oriented work, the teacher-scholar does not function as the disembodied, heroic pedagogue after whom teachers are to model themselves. Instead, the teacher-scholar is reflective about his or her specific, embodied location and the contexts he or she works within. Additionally, praxis-oriented work is developmental, not conclusive. The goal is not to come to final answers, but to participate in dialogue that has potential to change the teacher, the students, and the field (Haswell 1991). Finally, praxis-oriented scholarship need not look like scholarship that is already valued in the discipline; indeed, it can change the way we understand scholarship.

It is not difficult to find examples of such work. Carmen Luke and Jennifer Gore's collection *Feminisms and Critical Pedagogy,* for instance, offers an enabling "intervention" in the discourse of the critical pedagogy magister by focusing, as they point out in their introduction to the volume, on readings of critical pedagogy arrived at out of the writers' specific positions, locations, and identities as women in education (1992, 3). Of course, one might ask, why do this work in scholarship at all; doesn't it simply reinforce the current system whereby scholarship remains privileged over teaching? They argue, though, that given the "text-centered logos" of all institutionalized pedagogy, it makes sense to intervene from within, and to create a book that will allow women's voices to speak in sites traditionally dominated by male voices. In this way, then, they work at once within and against the tradition of critical pedagogy, most notably examining this discourse by tracing it in relation to "specific practices and embodied relations in classrooms" (4). In doing so, they not only make the classroom a site of theory, but also show how classroom experience can exert useful pressure on the discourse of critical pedagogy—complicating, critiquing, and extending it. They show, in other words, how the teacher can instruct the scholar.

Praxis-oriented pedagogy scholarship also emphasizes theory-work as process. As Ferry writes, "because the context that creates theory always changes, theory occurs in a constant of becoming rather than as a totalizing narrative" (1998, 17). In *Composing Critical Pedagogies,* Amy Lee seeks to challenge the notion that one can simply "take a position" or "name oneself a progressive educator" and instead to highlight the tangible and material work of teaching by offering a "critical portfolio of one teacher's (ongoing) process of coming to a specific version of critical pedagogy in the teaching of writing" (2000, 5). Similarly, Gallagher builds his argument in *Radical Departures* out of the notion that pedagogy cannot be "'given' by 'experts' to 'practitioners'" (2002, xxii). He thus offers narratives designed to represent the progressive pedagogy for which he argues in specific sites and enacted by particular subjects, to provide material "for teachers and researchers to engage with." His narratives do not simply show what his visions look like in practice, but work in dialogue with them, challenging and questioning them, as much as confirming them. In this way, then, praxis-oriented scholarship is not intended to be conclusive, to provide final answers, but rather to enrich the dialogue and to invite others into the conversation.

As I've noted above, Minter and Goodburn's collection *Composition, Pedagogy, and the Scholarship of Teaching* offers a useful intervention and extension of more traditional Carnegie-based scholarship-of-teaching discourse. While they are interested in helping teachers document their work for prospective employers, tenure-review committees, and administrators, they are equally interested in the potential of teacher research and documentation to facilitate reflection on one's professional commitments and to enable both teacher and program development (xviii). They refuse to separate "practical" from "intellectual" issues. For instance, as Peggy O'Neill describes her process of composing a teaching portfolio, she also considers the complicated contexts informing the construction of this "self" to be confessed and made public to a search committee. And as they promote a range of documentation practices, many of the contributors critique the problematic assumptions inherent in local and national calls to document teaching (xviii). In so doing, they offer useful examples of *reflexively* documenting and inquiring into our pedagogies.

Teaching Scholarship Differently

In addition to changing the way we compose pedagogy scholarship, we need also to alter the way we introduce and teach it to others. As composition's body of scholarship grows, it becomes easy to conflate the research—books, journals, and articles—with the discipline. And certainly, if we abide by the traditional conception of the discipline, which centers on a body of knowledge, this makes good sense. However, if we seek to enact a field that places engagement with teachers and students at its center, then the scholarship becomes one contributor to the conversation—not knowledge to acquire for disciplinary entry.

As I've discussed here and in the last chapter, as much as we have moved beyond a "reading as acquisition" model in English studies, teacher training has remained focused primarily on consumption, whether that means acquiring a set of practices or a body of theory. But if we are to change the way we teach the next generation to engage pedagogy—to practice teaching—then we must alter the way we teach the scholarship on teaching.

To conclude this chapter, I will offer several activities designed to promote praxis-oriented pedagogical inquiry, as well as examples of how these might play out in the classroom. These are not intended to be models; there are multiple ways of enacting this work, and they should be worked out within each pedagogical context. Rather, they illustrate the process of one group of learners negotiating pedagogical inquiry as praxis.

Reading and Writing to Develop

Since ideally composition scholarship is more process- than acquisition-focused, it makes sense to help new and future teachers *read toward development*—not for totalizing visions or what-works practices—but for the sake of questioning, challenging, discussing. We can, in other words, help students to *read as re-*

flexive teachers, to ask some of the following questions: What visions and values are being espoused? What is the role of the teacher? of the student? How is the writer situated as a teacher? What is the pedagogy of the writer's argument? What are the implications of this article for my classroom? What, given my experience as a teacher (or student), do I have to "say back" to this article? How does my concrete experience extend or complicate the message here?

In addition to adding pedagogy scholarship to our teacher-preparation sites, we can also *expand the range of texts we "count" as pedagogical scholarship.* For instance, students might be invited to visit the classrooms of other teachers—and to engage in dialogue with them—in order to consider the pedagogical assumptions and values present, the relationship between aims and enactments, and the contributions these acts make to the discipline (I discuss the practice of classroom visits in great detail in Chapter 4). Or students might be asked to study writing textbooks, bringing to bear the same critical questions they would ask of more traditional "scholarship." Lee puts it well: "Rather than naming teaching as 'practice' and research as 'theory,' I am suggesting we reconceptualize our work as teachers and scholars in order to prioritize action and reflection in both capacities" (2000, 101).

This leads me to a second important practice for praxis-oriented inquiry: *writing to develop.* The writing we assign needs to foster a dynamic interaction among scholarly texts, pedagogical sites, and teachers' ideas and interests. The kind of writing to develop that I advocate is not so different from the kind of writing to discover promoted in most process-based pedagogies. The idea is that students use writing as an opportunity to examine and engage in current conversations, to bring together various components of their doctoral preparation (scholarship and teaching, for instance), and to move toward making a contribution—to get situated—as teacher-scholars in the field.

Of course, helping students to *write as reflexive teachers* means opening up the kinds of composing that we usually consider "scholarly" to include forms like (process-oriented) teaching statements, reflective journals, a letter to a teacher-scholar or a co-teacher, and teaching portfolios. While we in composition often rely on forms that include personal reflection, we may need to educate others (including students) that this writing is indeed scholarly and rigorous, even if it doesn't display finished knowledge or look like a traditional disciplinary contribution. For instance, as I recently developed a course for English education majors on composition theory and practices, I was warned by one member of the majors committee that some might read my assignments (which did not include a traditional research paper) as not rigorous and too dependent upon "personal" writing. I was surprised at the remark, since I had not considered the assignments personal, but rather a way to integrate multiple methods of classroom research, personal reflection, and response to published articles. What I needed to do, I realized, was to highlight the ways in which students were doing research and relying on theoretical perspectives, even if they didn't look familiar to more traditional scholars.

While writing that allows students to link their classroom work to their scholarly study would ideally take place in every graduate classroom, my point here is that students benefit from writing in careful, reflective, and critical ways about their pedagogical ideas, experiences, and questions. The goal is not to train them as future "pedagogy scholars," but to begin part of a lifelong practice of critical reflection on teaching that takes place in dialogue with others—whether in the hallway, in journals, or in the classroom.

One Version

In order to highlight pedagogical inquiry as a praxis—a theoretical and practical act—I invite my M.A. composition theory students to lead the class in a "pedagogy facilitation." I set it up in this way:

> The aim of the pedagogy facilitation is twofold. First, it allows you to gain experience leading us in an activity. This activity could be one you draw from your own experience as a student, from our readings, or from the textbook you analyzed. It could also be something you create. Second, it's designed to give us all

an opportunity to critically reflect on that pedagogical practice. As teachers, we often give assignments without experiencing them for ourselves, or analyzing the "version of reality" (Berlin 1987) they promote. Here we can talk about our experiences as students. But we can also reflect, as teachers and scholars, on the assumptions, values, limits, and possibilities of that particular practice (a full list of questions is included in Appendix A).

In her facilitation, one student, Darby, chose to focus on the syllabus she'd constructed for her first-year writing class. In her handout, she immediately challenges the naturalized conception of a syllabus as simply a contract or statement of the teacher's goals and objectives, describing it as a more complex document. She first reflects on the syllabi she has encountered as a student:

> I found myself reading each syllabus not only as a syllabus, but also as a thumbnail sketch of the professor. I would note the choice of font, the logic of the organization, the tone of the written comments, the professor's availability. Most of all I tried to intuit the professor's standards; how intellectually sophisticated he or she was, how sophisticated I would need to be. Although these miniature evaluations took place on an almost subconscious level, the syllabus carried a good deal of emotional and mental weight. The syllabus had the power to create anxiety (even panic), to stimulate anticipation and excitement, or to frustrate even before the course really started. (Arant 2003a)

Now, she writes, she is responsible for creating her own syllabus. She describes looking through the "model" syllabi she has been given by friends. "My priority is to develop a clean document, first of all, which is well-organized and not unnecessarily complicated. [. . .] I try to write clearly and without a discernable 'tone' avoiding both severity and warmth. I list my goals, the books I'm assigning, my rules and expectations. [. . .] But I do not know (yet) how to read my own syllabus; I do not know what pedagogy is presented in this document, largely because I do not know what pedagogy I use. What does the syllabus really tell my students?"

Darby invited us to help her critically reflect on her syllabus, asking the following questions: How are the students positioned? How do I position myself? What are the students expected to know and do? How is writing situated? As an academic skill, a method of self-discovery, a tool for the real world? A stimulating discussion of Darby's syllabus followed, particularly as we noted the way in which Darby's authoritative voice seemed to shift throughout the document. Sometimes she referred to herself and students as a collective "we," sometimes she distanced herself from them (e.g., "students will . . .") and tellingly, in the plagiarism section, she referred to herself in third person ("the instructor may deem it necessary . . ."). Interestingly, Andrea pointed to a similar practice in my own syllabus, noting that my voice shifted significantly in the plagiarism section—a component we are now required at my university to include, and with which I feel discomfort. As a result of these observations, a productive discussion ensued about the ambivalence Darby felt as a young, new, female instructor—still a student herself—in attempting both to establish her authority and to create a community in the classroom.

During her facilitation, I became aware that Darby seemed already to have learned that part of reflexive pedagogical inquiry is knowing what questions to ask; but another part is inviting others to answer those questions alongside her. That is, by opening up her syllabus to us, we were able to talk about our multiple readings, as well as the institutional, personal, and social pressures surrounding the composition of such a document. While we certainly engaged in a scholarly reading of Darby's syllabus, we were not "peer reviewing" it for certain, predetermined criteria. Rather, we collectively helped her to make visible her goals, and to articulate the ways in which her visions and practices meshed (or did not).

Another way I invite students to participate in pedagogical inquiry is to analyze a first-year writing textbook. Here students are asked to consider the pedagogy implicit (or explicit) in the book: how are writing and language understood? How are the teacher, student, and editors positioned in relation to one another? How is student writing used in the book, and how do we make sense of this choice? Would you use this book in your first-year class? Why or why not? (The full assignment is included in Appendix B).

I have found that this assignment not only allows students to critically examine what is often naturalized—the epistemology, assumptions, and values that inform a book—but also helps them to position themselves as teachers, to place their own beliefs in dialogue with those espoused in the textbook. Even those students who have never taught are able to consider, as they make explicit the pedagogy of the book, where the ideas do or do not resonate with their own values and assumptions. I return to Darby's work, to show her ongoing process of development. In her analysis of Gallagher and Lee's *Writers at Work: Invitations,* she writes:

> I would certainly teach this book because it matches the peda-gogy that I am beginning to form for myself: one that values dialogue, community, flexibility to recognize and respond to vary-ing rhetorical contexts, and a critical alertness to one's position as writer and reader. This text is especially compelling to me because it gets students (writers!) to interrogate their own posi-tions through precise, pointed questions that follow almost ev-ery exercise. The questions are the same ones I seek to answer about my own writing and my own approach to teaching writ-ing. Furthermore, they instill a sense of ownership in the writer as he or she learns to write beyond the expected answers. I am still learning to do this, to ask myself, what do I really *think* about a certain issue? And, perhaps more important, to ask my-self the harder question of why. (Arant 2003b)

Here it is clear not only that Darby is able to articulate the cen-tral values and questions of *Writers at Work,* but also that she can discuss them in relation to her own developing pedagogy (which she can also articulate here).

Having discovered interesting threads in her facilitation and analysis, Darby decided to compose a teaching portfolio for her final project, which would allow her to create a new syllabus that better represents her current pedagogical beliefs, as well as reflective material on her ever-evolving teaching self. When I met with her to discuss this project, I mentioned that she could use it to document her teaching for Ph.D. program applications. In the end, though, we decided that this would limit the project at this moment, a time when she wanted to explore the complexities, contradictions, and uncertainties in her teaching—not yet present herself to a "judging" body. As Ray reminds us, knowledge making in composition is a "rhetorical act, which takes on many forms, depending on individual researchers, their audience and purpose" (1993, 137). Here Darby chose a teaching portfolio over a traditional seminar paper, and she chose to write more for her colleagues—fellow developing teachers—than for an audience that would more explicitly evaluate and judge her work. As Chris Anson and Deanna Dannels write, "too often high evaluations are given to teaching portfolios that display teaching in the slickest, least insightful or probing ways" (2002, 92). Darby was more interested in a portfolio that would reflect the complicated realities of teaching—the partiality of her own knowledge, the dynamic interactions between herself and students, the ongoing and often unanswerable questions, than she was in presenting a "slick" product. She also decided to construct the portfolio as a Web site, which will not only show her ongoing development and allow her to easily make revisions, but will also be a public document—challenging the notion that teaching is private.

Already, then, Darby is engaged in praxis-oriented pedagogical inquiry, working toward studying her teaching not to produce conclusive findings or final visions, but to participate in ongoing reflection and revision. In the next chapter, I will focus more closely on another writing practice—the learning narrative—that helps to challenge the notion of the finished professor and also to highlight the knowledge that all new teachers bring to the classroom, by virtue of their experience as students.

Appendix A

Facilitation Guidelines

The aim of the pedagogy facilitation is twofold. First, it allows you to gain experience (in a safe setting) leading us in an activity. This activity could be one you draw from your own experience as a student, from our readings, or from the textbook you analyzed. It could also be something you create. Second, it's designed to give us all an opportunity to critically reflect on that pedagogical practice. As teachers, we often give assignments without experiencing them for ourselves, or analyzing the "version of reality" (Berlin 1987) they promote. Here we can talk about our experiences as students. But we can also reflect, as teachers and scholars, on the assumptions, values, limits, and possibilities of that particular practice.

Some questions we might consider:

- ◆ What did this assignment enable for us as writers/readers/thinkers?

- ◆ What felt enabling about it? constraining? As teachers, are we comfortable with those aspects?

- ◆ How does the practice position the student? the teacher?

- ◆ What is it designed to help students know, be able to do?

- ◆ What seem to be the assumptions about the teaching of writing informing this practice?

- ◆ How does this practice seem informed by particular theory we've read? How do our experiences "speak back" to this theory?

- ◆ Would we use this practice as teachers? Why or why not?

I am also open to other "variations" of this assignment. Please check with me if you have an alternate idea.

Appendix B

Textbook Analysis

Lester Faigley contends that writing textbooks "reflect teachers' and program directors' decisions about how writing should be represented to students" (1992, 133). Indeed, choosing a textbook is both a theoretical and a political act. For this short (5- to 7-page) assignment, I'd like you to analyze a first-year writing textbook. In doing so, keep in mind that textbooks can be seen to have two pedagogies: (1) the pedagogy argued for (what approach is being promoted) and (2) the pedagogy of the argument (*how* the approach is promoted) (Gore 1993). So I'd like you to analyze the textbook with an eye toward both of those pedagogies, with the following questions in mind:

- ◆ According to this textbook, what is the purpose of a writing course? (Is it to prepare students to write academic discourse, to empower them as writers, to help them become critical thinkers?)

CHAPTER TWO

◆ How is language/writing understood? What ends does it serve?

◆ How are students, their needs, their interests articulated?

◆ What is the role of the writing teacher?

◆ What role do the editors of the book play? (Are they friendly guides, firm authorities?)

◆ How do the readings in the book function? What kinds of readings are used? Are they models? Are they texts to engage and/or challenge?

◆ Is there student writing in the book? What purpose does it serve?

◆ Are there detailed assignments/exercises provided? What do they tell you about the pedagogy being promoted?

◆ How does the organization of the text function? What does it tell you about the book's pedagogy?

◆ Do you see contradictions in the text? (Between what is argued for and the way the argument is articulated? Are there ideas about writing that don't mesh with one another?)

◆ How does this book's pedagogy work in relation to your own? What do you find innovative, interesting about the book? What troubles you?

◆ Would you teach this book? Why? Would you like this book as a student? Why?

You need not address all of these questions. Please feel free, too, to pursue one issue/line of inquiry in more depth.

The Teacher as Trainee

*It is rare that we take or make the time, or are rewarded
for efforts that are primarily a collecting of the already-
said, or a re-assembling of what we have read or heard.
[. . .] Indeed, the process of collecting and re-assembling
leaves open the possibility for rupture, for interrupting
our current regimes and practices, perhaps even more so
than the constant attempts to innovate beyond what we
know. That is, in always looking forward, it is easy to
accept what is behind as a given.*

JENNIFER GORE, *The Struggle for Pedagogies*

In the previous chapters, I've described a tendency to position
pedagogy either as a body of knowledge to be mastered or a set
of skills to be acquired. In this chapter, I'll focus on another root
metaphor that perpetuates this limited conception of pedagogy:
teacher as trainee. Teacher-preparation models that position the
teacher as trainee are tied to what Delandshere and Petrosky
(1994) call an "essentialist" approach to teacher education. The
terms are familiar enough: the process of teaching and learning is
reduced to a checklist of skills and knowledge, such that the sum
of these components is presumed to equal readiness to teach
(McWilliam 1994; McLean 1999). Here the teacher-training site
is considered the sole provider of one's pedagogy, with the new
teacher positioned as either a blank slate—without pedagogical
interests, assumptions, and values of his or her own—or as
wrongly inscribed—in need of pedagogical "conversion." As Joy
Ritchie and David Wilson have it, "colleges of education [and, I
would add, teacher preparation in doctoral programs] have often presented the teacher as a rational agent whose pedagogical

decisions emerge from a single intellectual position provided by teacher education" (2000, 11).

One of the greatest consequences of positioning the teacher as "trainee," waiting to be "filled up" by the teacher-preparation site, is that the pedagogical visions and values with which the learner enters the program are ignored. Instead, beginning teachers are expected to function as "deliverers of other people's policies, purveyors of other people's values, puppets moving to strings that are always manipulated by others" (Ruddick 1992, 165). While this model is certainly called into question by recent scholarship on pedagogy, particularly the "critical" versions, there are many institutional contexts that ensure its preservation (for both K–12 teachers and teaching assistants).

Take, for instance, the institutional contexts surrounding most first-year writing programs. All too often, part-time teachers of composition are hired just weeks before the semester, and graduate students need to "become" teaching assistants in a matter of weeks or days. Consequently, it isn't surprising that efficiency-based training models, or what Latterell calls "what works" approaches, in which teachers are handed a prepackaged pedagogy (text, master syllabus, pretested assignments, etc.) continue to dominate teacher education (Latterell 1996; Crowley 1998; Stenberg and Lee 2002; Tremmel 1994). In fact, as Robert Tremmel argues, "limited resources and the low esteem in which many compositionists are held by their institutions and departments ensure that these bad things still happen—even with good people in charge" (1994, 45).

Even when more time and resources are dedicated to teacher preparation, new teachers are often still positioned as "empty vessels" who are in some way deficient—needing either new knowledges or new skills. In fact, we see examples of this even in seemingly "progressive" programs. Bishop's ethnography *Something Old, Something New* traces teachers' participation in process-oriented programs informed by the Bay Area Writing Project model, which ultimately functioned, she contends, to "convert" teachers' identities and pedagogies to a predetermined model. She writes, "[T]he teacher of a convergent theory writing pedagogy classroom [. . .] might be working unabashedly to change teachers' behaviors and teachers' identities, and might also be working to change teachers' institutions by so changing the teachers" (1990, xiv). Similarly, in "Resisting the Faith: Conversion, Resistance, and the Training of Teachers," Welch (1993) describes her experience in a social-constructionist teacher-training program where professors exhibited a Foucauldian "will to truth," enlightening their students to the one "true" and "critical" way to teach. New teachers were regarded not only as lacking legitimate pedagogical visions of their own, but also as working out of a state of false consciousness that the teaching course and its already-converted professors could "cure." In this way, the program functioned as a "reorientation" (Giroux and McLaren 1986), replacing the new teacher's (presumably) "traditional" ideas with "critical" knowledge. In both cases the problem is not so much that these programs espoused a (political) vision—all programs do—but rather that the pedagogy of the teacher-training program was not left open to reflection or critique, nor were students positioned as having valid insights and ideas that might work in dialogue with, or even alter, those ideals. Moreover, both kinds of programs seem to assume that acquisition of knowledge—whether "critical" or methodological—will result in effective practices and affective confidence, squelching any teacher doubts, frustrations, or questions.

In this chapter I seek to challenge the "teacher-as-trainee" metaphor by reconceiving the (new) teacher as a complex subject who brings a complicated pedagogical history to the classroom. My first goal is to write the learner back into the professor, insisting that our histories as students play a significant role in our subject-formation as professors. With Stephen Brookfield I agree that while we may "espouse philosophies of teaching that we have learned from formal study" the "most significant, most deeply embedded influences that operate on us are the images, models, and conceptions of teaching derived from our own experience as learners" (1995, 49).

Second, I argue against the notion that we can finally be trained as teachers; I contend that reflecting on our histories as learners is not just important for "new" teachers, but is crucial for our continuing development. In the same way that unlearning racism or sexism requires an ongoing examination of the relationship between our lives and the cultures that form us, we cannot finally "move beyond" the contexts in which we have learned. Instead, I would argue that we benefit from ongoing dialogue between the pedagogies from which we've learned and the pedagogies we seek to enact. In what follows, then, I explore the contexts of, and promote the practice of, reflexive learner narratives, which require continuing analysis of one's history as a student in relation to one's beliefs, values, and practices as a teacher. I also advance the praxis of learner narratives from the perspective of the teacher, demonstrating that learning moments—moments of perplexity, disorientation, even chaos—can lead, upon reflection and inquiry, to new pedagogical possibilities.

(Re)learning Learning Narratives: Prolonging the Uncertainty

The practice of sharing learning stories, whether formally or informally, has long been a component of teacher-education discourse. Until recently, however, stories of teaching and learning have typically been discounted as merely anecdotal, romanticized, or untheoretical. Now, poststructuralist conceptions of experience, language, and subjectivity require us to reconceive stories as central to the process of teacher development—it is, as S. Vianne McLean reminds us, "not our concrete experiences that shape our sense of identity, but the stories we tell ourselves (and exchange with other people) about those experiences" (1999, 78). Consequently, a growing body of education and composition scholarship makes story a subject of intellectual inquiry in pedagogical research (McLean 1999; Carter 1993; Brunner 1994; Clandinin 1992; Ritchie and Wilson 2000; Gallagher, Gray, and Stenberg 2002; Welch 1997; Lee 2000; Qualley 1997; Kameen 2000). In fact, Ritchie and Wilson argue that an "evolution in the use of narrative" is now underway, with stories serving as "critical instruments" (in Teresa de Lauretis's phrase) for "illuminating the ideologies" by which our lives and teaching practices are composed (21).

Despite this increase in use, and reconception in purpose, of teaching and learning stories, it is important to note, as McLean does, that the *"pedagogy* of stories in teacher education still is in its infancy"* (1999, 83; my emphasis). In other words, the question of *how* we employ, respond to, and construct stories in teacher education sites has not yet been sufficiently examined. These are crucial concerns if we hope to prevent narratives from becoming another mechanism for teacher correction and training.

Ideally, the learner narrative is used as a touchstone to which the developing teacher may continually return as he or she encounters a range of pedagogical theory, such that "the story becomes part of the context by which to make sense of theory, and vice versa" (McLean 1999, 83). If learner narratives are to function critically, however, it is important to keep an eye on the potential influence of the normative training model, which employs learner stories as a site for correction. Here, the teacher educator occupies a position of "trainer" and "knower" in relation to the narrator, and responds by offering the "real" meaning or authorizing an interpretation that will lead the new teacher to conform to a predetermined vision. Positioning the new teacher as "trainee" in need of the teacher educators' "reading" and "answer" not only implies a lack of trust in the new teacher's interpretive strategies, but also impedes possibilities for the teacher educator to learn from the story.

As Ritchie and Wilson and D. Jean Clandinin (1992) demonstrate, in order for learner stories to function as sites of critical, collaborative inquiry, teacher educators need to actively reflect on *how* the stories function within their pedagogies. Drawing from their experience of engaging learner stories, Ritchie and Wilson demonstrate that it is all too easy to categorize stories in dualistic ways, either as "traditional" or "progressive," and thus to impose a reading on them that will lead students in a particular pedagogical direction (33). Clandinin highlights a similar tendency, as she describes her difficulty in responding to a new teacher's story that did not look as she expected or hoped it would: it relied heavily on quotations from experts, silenced her own voice, and seemed distanced from the students with whom this teacher worked (133). When she gave the new teacher her response, noting these characteristics, the teacher was initially angry with Clandinin and herself; eventually, though, the two were able to work in dialogue to consider what "institutional narratives" informed both of their responses, and how those contexts "shaped and constrained" what they hoped would be a collaborative learning moment between new and experienced teacher (133).

As Kathy Carter argues, "we must begin to ask what our stories [and our students' stories] are told in service of" (1993, 9) so as to avoid the tendency to smooth over student narratives, to impose single readings, or to categorize or label narratives in any final or fixed ways. In fact, Ritchie and Wilson remind us that within any pedagogy, a variety of epistemologies exist, "and from any one epistemology, a variety of pedagogies might be implied" (2000, 33). A pedagogy that works against training, then, needs to "prolong the uncertainty" (Brunner 1994, 47) of any story and its epistemological roots, instead helping students to engage the multiple layers and meanings stories make possible.

Indeed, I would argue that we have a very limited tolerance for ambiguity when it comes to learning narratives, a phenomenon we can see when examining responses to published learner narratives. I think, for instance, of my classmates', and later, students' responses to Michelle Payne's "Rend(er)ing Women's Authority in the Writing Classroom," in which she examines how her history as a woman in an emotionally abusive home (a crucial pedagogical site in the formation of the self, certainly) has impinged upon her conception and experience of authority as a teacher in the classroom. She reads her experience alongside calls for "student-centered" pedagogies, questioning the charge to "give up" her authority, when her authority has historically been in question. Crucially, she also demonstrates her awareness that making visible her struggles of teacher learning is accompanied by a particular risk:

> By sharing my personal experience, and certainly my feelings, I may be inviting someone to come along and determine I am unfit, unstable, too emotional to be in a position of power—that my presentation of efficiency and capability is exactly that, a presentation. (1994, 100)

That Payne names this a "risk" indicates to me that we have *not* learned, or at least that she does not trust us, to read narratives in which the teacher occupies the role of learner. In fact, we tend to use them to point to the deficits evident—the ways in which the teacher is not yet trained and disciplined. As Payne suggests, acknowledgment of being a teacher in process—and more, one who has been written on by (and is working to write against) the pedagogies of her past—puts her in danger of being read as someone not ready to teach, not ready to occupy professorial authority.

I saw this play out in a composition theory class (made up mostly of M.A. students and teachers) in which Payne's piece was assigned as an example of "teacher research." While this article certainly wasn't the only piece we read demonstrating a teacher theorizing out of her classroom, it was the only one that depicted a teacher feeling ambivalence about this role, showing teaching as an intellectual and psychological struggle. Of course, as I've shown above, Payne is fully aware that this kind of ambivalence is not usually allowed in academic writing. I read this articulation of her fear as both an attempt to highlight that which is exiled from "disciplinary work" and a strategic rhetorical move, teaching us how *not* to read it. Even so, it was received by several students just as Payne predicted. Instead of focusing on the mode of inquiry engaged, or discussing the questions and issues she raised, the discussion was limited to the psychological state of the author and her seeming "deficiency" as a teacher. One student said, "I just want to sit down with Michelle Payne and have a talk with her about how she's running that class!" Another remarked, "She's so passive. She seems so unconfident. Her students can probably sense that." Interestingly, when I taught this article in my own graduate class two years later, one student responded in an almost identical manner: blaming the individual for not feeling "confident" in her classroom, pointing out that the students could probably see through her "insecurities" and were thus taking advantage. In other words, Payne was understood as not yet having achieved the disposition of a "trained" and disciplined teacher: confident, assertive, and certain of her own visions and practices. This demonstrates just how deeply embedded is the notion of professor as finished knower, since a challenge to this subjectivity evokes not only blame but also anger.

We see a similar example of unwillingness on the part of readers to "prolong the uncertainty" in Giroux and McLaren's response to Elizabeth Ellsworth's article "Why Doesn't This Feel Empowering? Working through the Repressive Myths of Critical Pedagogy." Here Ellsworth describes her struggle to put into practice the prescriptions of critical pedagogy. Her piece argues that in the specific context of her class, abiding by the literature of critical pedagogy's "highly abstract language ('myths') of who we 'should' be and what 'should' be happening in our classroom" functioned only to reproduce the very conditions this "liberatory" discourse seeks to work against (1989, 91). She highlights her partiality as a critical teacher and ultimately argues that we cannot abide by fixed and finished notions of critical pedagogy.

In response to her learning narrative (first presented as a paper at the 1988 Critical Theory and Classroom Practice Conference), Giroux (1988a) and McLaren (1988) blame Ellsworth's "difficulty" in enacting critical pedagogy on her "disengagement" from, and misreading of, the tradition. McLaren goes so far as to contend that her pedagogical difficulty is attributable to her "inability to move beyond self-doubt" (72). Again, her learning narrative is read for deficiencies, and in this case, those include her presumed lack of understanding of critical pedagogy scholarship. The assumption seems to be that if she were properly trained—with the right knowledges—she would not work out of an exploratory, questioning stance.

Rather than using narratives as an occasion to diagnose the narrator, narrative inquiry should be used "to foster reflection and restorying on the part of *all* participants in the inquiry" (Clandinin 1992, 129; my emphasis). That is to say, the story can become an opportunity for both new and experienced teachers to reflect on their pedagogical beliefs and assumptions. Clandinin suggests that the teacher educator might add his or her reflective voice to the story by asking questions about why the story was told in the way it was, encouraging the writer to examine more deeply the "emotionality" attached to this way of storying events and to connect the story to other narratives (128). In addition, both teachers work to locate the social and institutional contexts that shaped the story—and, equally important, the response to it—as well as the ways the story might speak back to professional knowledge and to the situation in which it occurred.

I would contend, then, that we need to learn new ways of "prolonging the uncertainty" both as readers of student narratives and of published learning narratives—to increase our own comfort with ambiguity and uncertainty.

Story as Reflexive Inquiry

Prolonging the uncertainty is important not only for engaging learner narratives, but also for composing them. Gore argues that discourses can be seen to have two pedagogies: the pedagogy argued for (claims or arguments made) and the pedagogy of the argument (the process of knowledge evident within the argument itself) (1993, 5). As Brannon points out, the pedagogy argued for and the pedagogy of the argument of the teacher narratives we typically celebrate in both scholarly and popular cultural realms tend not to serve as a site for investigation into one's own teacher learning, but as a way to redeem teaching as a heroic practice and the teacher as a hero. They do not depict the teacher as struggling, or, if he or she is, the struggle is a means to a heroic end, when he or she emerges as the "rugged individual who works against all odds to make a difference" (think *Dangerous Minds, Music from the Heart, Stand and Deliver*) (1993, 459).

Even, then, as the field abides by poststructuralist resistance to grand narratives and unified subjectivity, (published) teacher narratives often promote (or are expected to promote) a neat and linear story told by a unified narrator. Any moments of messiness are to be cleaned up and polished by the story's end. The teacher is expected to discover or return to a unified and authoritative position—to show him- or herself as finally "trained" or "oriented." These narratives ultimately lead to closure, presenting the teacher as the victor—as finally finished learning or "training"—with the students benefiting from the teacher's decisiveness and rigor.[1]

One example of this tendency can be found in Giroux's "Who Writes in a Composition Class?" This text provides readers the rare opportunity to "see" Giroux in the classroom, as a teacher enacting the pedagogy for which he so often argues. He begins the piece by describing his typical classroom, in which his over-riding pedagogical project is "an attempt at majority democratic education" wherein students interrogate "the possibility of ad-dressing schooling as a site of ongoing struggle" over resistance, social transformation, and radical democracy (1995, 11). Giroux found, however, that his current pedagogical practices failed to "unsettle the kinds of social relations that characterize teacher-centered environments" (10). In fact, he discovered that he was only replicating the kinds of classrooms he wants to work against: students seemed intimidated by the language of theory; white males typically dominated conversation; and the students con-tinued to position Giroux as the authority, directing comments at him rather than their classmates.

From this experience, Giroux learned that there was a gap between his aims and enactments. As he puts it, "I reproduced the binarism of being politically enlightened in my theorizing and pedagogically wrong in my organization of concrete class rela-tions" (11). Consequently, he describes a new set of practices he employed; he made writing a more central component of the course, included more "student-centered" practices like collabo-rative assignments and self-evaluation, and rethought his own "politics of location" in the classroom. In the end, then, he re-emerges as the decisive teacher who is ultimately in *control* of his classroom; his commitment to his pedagogical vision has never wavered, and now his practices are better aligned with those ide-als. Both the critical teacher and the scholarship of critical peda-gogy remain intact.

While we do see a growing body of learning-oriented narra-tive work in composition (Lee 2000; Gallagher 2002; Qualley 1997; Welch 1993, 1997; Payne 1994; Kameen 2000), this por-trayal of the teacher as a learner—one who is exploratory, in the midst of change and revision—is still overshadowed by the more traditional "teacher-as-hero" model. I would contend that if we are to make learning narratives a crucial component of teacher education, we need to see examples of learners and learning nar-ratives in scholarly forums—not only to serve as examples, but to challenge the notion that experienced teachers are finished knowers.

Given the response to, and devalued status of, *teacher* learning narratives, it is not surprising that we have even fewer reflections written by teachers to examine their histories as *students*. It seems the research model has successfully excised the formative role the subject position of student plays in the development of professors. This is a significant omission, since, as Dan Lortie points out, by the time a teacher enters teacher education (or TA training), he or she has observed teachers for some thirteen thousand hours (qtd. in Ritchie and Wilson 2000, 32). If not deliberately studied, those experiences become naturalized, and the formative role they played—and continue to play throughout one's teaching career—are ignored.

If we seek to enact a "critical" mode of reflection, whereby teachers use story to examine their learning experiences as gendered, raced, classed subjects in order to consider how these moments shape their visions, values, and practices as teachers, then there can be no conclusive narratives. As McLean argues, "[N]o one can provide final answers, and no one comes to 'feel comfortable' with her identity because that identity is not a stable, fixed phenomenon, but something that shifts as the context changes" (1999, 76). This "critical" approach to teacher inquiry not only values uncertainty and ongoing inquiry but promotes examination of the dialogic relationship among our histories, present circumstances, commitments, investments, and institutional and cultural discourses about what it means to be a teacher (Britzman 1994, 8).

It is this kind of "critical" reflection that will help us to challenge the notion of (new) teacher as blank slate or "trainee," and which also aids experienced teachers in an ongoing reflection of the contexts that have shaped them. To this end, I am interested in the praxis of composing—in official and unofficial ways— student and learner[2] narratives. But I want to be clear that I am not promoting just any kind of student narratives. I am not promoting student inquiry that simply celebrates or regards with disdain the classrooms in which one learned, only to insist (with relief) that one has not become one's former professors. As two respondents note in Allen's survey, "My courses illustrated how bad teaching could be"; "[T]hey taught me to be a good teacher by showing me how not to be a bad one" (1968, 57). This is too simple. It suggests that there is simply "bad" teaching and "good" teaching, and that by not engaging in certain practices, or doing what our teachers did, we can avoid "bad" teaching. As I see it, the aim of a student inquiry isn't to finally condemn or praise our past classrooms. Rather, it is to examine how they have shaped us, to make visible what might, at the time, have seemed natural. The narratives I have in mind are not intended to lead to closure, to teach a fixed or final "lesson" that can be mastered. Instead, I want to argue for student narratives that rely on *reflexive inquiry*.

Reflexive inquiry has long been part of the tradition of composition and (some versions of) critical pedagogy; it began with John Dewey and has been appropriated and extended in the work of Paulo Freire, Donald Murray, Louise Wetherbee Phelps, Ann Berthoff, Donna Qualley, Jennifer Gore, Amy Lee, and Chris Gallagher. We also see discussions of critical reflection in the work of education scholars such as Donald Schön, Diane Brunner, Kenneth Zeichner and D. P. Liston, and Maxine Greene. My conception of reflexive inquiry into student histories borrows from their collection of work, and maintains these characteristics:

◆ Engaging in reflexive inquiry requires a "learner's stance," a stance that, as Qualley has it, "names itself in the here and now, [. . .] can explain how it came to be, but remains open to the possibility of further complication and change" (1997, 2). A learner's stance, however, is different from a perspective. It can't simply be claimed, but requires a deliberate decision to critically examine the present in light of the past—with an eye toward revision.

◆ It creates a dialogue between two sites—the classroom in which one learned and that in which one teaches—and two subject-positions—student and teacher—in order to enable the teacher to see his or her present actions and subject position anew.

◆ It refuses closure or "final readings," since when we return to a text, it is never the same text, nor are we the same readers. This means that we don't simply visit these classrooms once, but that we keep returning to them: we keep learning from them. As Qualley names it, "reflexivity is a response triggered by a dialectical engagement with the other [. . .] by dialectical, I mean an engagement that is ongoing and recursive as opposed to a single, momentary encounter" (11).

♦ It requires a *self*-reflexivity, such that as one examines a learning moment, he or she asks questions not only about what was being studied and how, but how his or her own subjectivity played a role in that meaning making. As Gallagher states it, "To study reflexively is to inquire into the situatedness not only of the object of study, but also of the inquirers" (2002, xvii).

Scholars like Nancy Welch and Min-Zhan Lu have already begun the work of reflexive inquiry into their histories as learners. Lu's "From Silence to Words" examines her education in China, and the dissonance she experienced between the discourse of home and school. Lu was taught that acquiring the discourse of the dominant was a mode of survival, a way to seek alliance with the dominant group and thus to survive "the whirlpool of cultural currents" surrounding her (1987, 444). Consequently, she learned to be passive in her use of language, a bystander— not a participant—in discussion. Examining her roles as both a mother to a daughter experiencing a similar dissonance and as a teacher of writing, Lu strives now to look for ways in which this metaphor of language as a survival tool continues to crop up. She wants to work against the assumption that we are (or she is) beyond such a view of language, striving instead to use the classroom to "moderate the currents, but [to teach students] from the beginning to struggle" (447). The narrative works, in the end, to describe how the complexity of the circumstances in which she grew up serves now to keep her "from losing sight of the effort and choices involved in reading or writing with and through a discourse" (447). It is a complexity she wants neither to forget nor to overcome, but to continue to use in her teaching.

Welch's aforementioned "Resisting the Faith: Conversion, Resistance, and the Training of Teachers" shares with Lu's piece a commitment to learning from a complex (indeed, even painful) education experience. While Welch ultimately resists the pedagogy enacted and ideology espoused in this "conversion" course (and chooses to leave that university), what interests me is that by placing the two sites of learning in dialogue, Welch comes to see the beliefs about writing and teaching that she came with not as natural, but as assumptions. Though she (physically) returned to where she came from, she returned with a different vision. "I didn't realize how much I had learned and changed—not through converting to a given model but through working to identify and question it—a process that necessarily meant I must identify and question the model that was once my own" (1993, 398). Like Lu, Welch wants to make use of the space between embracing and rejecting, which allows for an ongoing questioning and revising of one's classroom.

Reflexive narratives also differ from other models in that they are not intended to offer final or complete renderings of the self as subject. Instead, they provide opportunities to theorize a particular moment, to dialogue with it, and to examine possibilities for change. For instance, the point of Payne's "Rend(er)ing Women's Authority in the Writing Classroom" is not to resolve that she cannot practice the pedagogy she values, because her social location will not allow it. Instead, her narrative makes visible that which is often overlooked in classrooms and in scholarship of "progressive" pedagogies in such a way that offers her choices. As Ritchie and Wilson argue, once a teacher has come to understand how he or she resides at the "intersections of various educational, gender, and social class ideologies" he or she is then allowed to make better choices about who he or she "will be" as a teacher, about what "identity [he or she will] choose to perform" (1994, 14).

Equally important is that Payne also refuses to "close" her text with neat conclusions or lessons. Instead, she raises questions that cannot be answered, that will have to be considered and reconsidered as she meets each new group of students, and as she, as a subject, changes along with her students. Her essay provides just one example of the way teacher narratives have evolved from neat and conclusive tales to complex renderings of classroom moments in which teachers demonstrate their ongoing learning, and the contexts—present and past—that inform it (see also Ellsworth 1989; Orner 1992; Lee 2000; Gallagher 2002; Welch 1993, 1997; Ritchie and Wilson 2000).

Following in the tradition of Lu, Welch, and Payne, and aiming to enact the kind of inquiry I have described above, I turn now to a narrative from my own history as a student. In order to show the process of reflexive inquiry, I have sought to represent two positions—my self as teacher and my self as student—in dialogue. My aim is to show my process of *teacher* learning as I read and respond to my student narrative. Thus, I have composed the story in two stages. The student narrative is the result of many tellings, the first of which began as a response paper during my first year of graduate school. It has been extended and rethought many times—especially as it has been responded to by insightful readers—as I have come to see it anew. The sections in italics are a more recent addition, demonstrating the questions, uncertainties, and insights that come from these student rememberings. From the teaching standpoint, another narrative emerges—one that parallels, complicates, and is complicated by my student story. Here, I hope to show the ongoing dialogue between past and present, as well as what is possible when I bring my "student" insights to bear on my current pedagogy.

Bridging the Teacher and the Learner: A Dialogue between Selves

It was the fall of my junior year. Just the semester before, I had changed my major from journalism to English, having discovered a field in which my writing could be studied, and where texts were understood to do important cultural work; indeed, I came to see that *my* texts could work on culture. Like many English majors during the early 1990s, I was part of a newly revised curriculum that shifted from "the study of texts as containers of meaning to a study of the critical thinking process by which writers and readers activate meaning through language" (Drake Univ. Dept. of English, "Curriculum Rationale" 2). No longer organized around periods, authors, and professors' specialties, the program, according to its Web site, sought to engage "in the study of the power of language to mediate relations between people and the world around them."

In addition to altering the approach to texts, this curriculum also changed the work that goes on in classrooms. In these classrooms, the subject matter no longer occupied the central position, since transmitting the "right" information seemed to matter less than the questions asked of and the activities engaged with students. Here, the focus was on students—we led discussions, we read one another's papers, we were asked to pursue "projects" (which I soon came to understand were different from papers, written to demonstrate mastery to the teacher). We were, it seemed, expected to be largely responsible for our learning, and even more, to enable the learning of others—including the teachers. Consequently, I began to rethink what I once believed to be "normal" practices and positions, where the teacher occupied a central role as knower and "corrector" of student knowledge.

As part of the "new" major in English, I was also afforded the opportunity to "concentrate" in an interdisciplinary project like cultural studies, multicultural studies, or women's studies. I was immediately drawn to cultural studies' emphasis on texts not usually privileged in academic sites, for the way it allowed me to link what I learned in the classroom to the culture in which I lived. I was excited to discover that any text could be critically examined and read, studied as a product—or even a producer— of culture, and further, that culture as we know it—the familiar, the commonsense—does not have to exist as it does.

This notion was strengthened through my discovery of a new community of feminist writers with whose projects I identified. Michelle Cliff, Jane Tompkins, and Trinh Minh-ha described their struggles as writers to speak both within and against dominant, masculine discourse. Their work spoke loudly to me; it resonated with my life experience. A white, Protestant young woman raised in the Midwest, I had learned the path to "acceptance" well: be respectful, be nice, be quiet. Be careful about speaking up. When you disagree be careful not to offend, insult.

But they also taught me that even within this new academic discourse community that I found so liberating and exciting, there were rules for acceptance, and that for feminist scholars, a tricky negotiation is often required. As Tompkins puts it, "To adhere to the conventions is to uphold a male standard of rationality that militates against women's being recognized as culturally legitimate sources of knowledge. To break with convention is to risk not being heard at all" (1991, 1081). As I tried on my new role of "theorist" or "cultural critic," I struggled with this notion of "legitimacy" at the same time I wrote about it, critiqued it. I had a project—one in which I was highly invested, one which was tied not only to myself as "intellectual" but to my social location and life history as a gendered subject. I began to voice what once seemed natural—silence, goodness, passivity—and to tie these "characteristics" to cultural norms and values. I began to feel a sense of agency, even as I became increasingly aware of all that constrains and disciplines women's voices.

I was thrilled, then, when the professor who helped me begin this project suggested I register for the course Rhetorics of Knowledge, which he would be teaching along with another professor from the rhetoric and communications department. The course would allow me an opportunity to continue to pursue the project I'd begun in his class, he told me. The focus of Rhetorics of Knowledge was intentionally broad, to allow students from both English and rhetoric to investigate modes of knowing in their respective fields. Looking back, I think most of us would have had difficulty describing what the class was "about." The course texts were quite varied—from Foucault's *Discipline and Punish* to excerpts from Bonnie Spanier's *Impartial Science: A Gender Ideology in Molecular Biology* to Tompkins's "'Indians': Textualism, Morality, and the Problem of History." Here, the focus was less on a commonality among texts, and more on a shared approach to engaging and examining them.

I entered the course with much optimism and anticipation. But I also did so with some hesitancy, because in addition to the "official" accounts of the new cultural studies program, and along with (and probably informing) my individual attachments to it, were the unofficial stories—the way the program was talked about by students and professors in the hallways and after class. Though only recently developed, the program was already being touted as highly "rigorous," relying on theoretical texts and pedagogical approaches often reserved for graduate courses. While this was exciting, it was also intimidating. Would I measure up? What would it require to succeed in such a climate?

As I reflect on the conflicting feelings I experienced as a student—the excitement about pursuing a project in a classroom that claimed to value students' work and fear that I would somehow not fit in, that my project (my self?) might not really be

sanctioned—I am led to consider the complexity of my peda-
gogical goals that function in the name of student "empower-
ment" or "liberation." I think, for instance, of the look of
puzzlement and skepticism on the face of one writer in my first-
year composition class, when I asked her: What do you want to
write about? I think of how, sometimes, despite my best inten-
tions, I hear students working in groups say to each other: Now,
what is it you think she wants? They know that even in a class-
room that claims to value their ideas, questions, and projects,
there are rules, constraints. As much as "student-centered" class-
rooms might enable pedagogical freedoms, they also—like all
pedagogies—rely on discipline and (self-) regulation. As Gore
contends, there is always an ethical aspect to any pedagogy that
determines the "being to which we aspire" (1993, 63). Who did
my teachers want me to be? Who do I want my students to be?

On the first day of Rhetorics of Knowledge, we (about fifteen English and rhetoric majors, mostly juniors) were told that
the course would examine how knowledge is produced and disciplined, and that our own textual inquiries—as much as the texts
we studied—would occupy the center of the course. The writing
workload, on top of the reading, seemed overwhelming: two "traditional" papers, three Storyspace documents, and an in-class
presentation. The professors explained that Storyspace, a
hypertextual word-processing program, would be used as a means
to interrupt traditional writing practices. The software allows
one to write in a nonlinear, layered fashion by composing in
"boxes" which can be linked to one another to create multiple
paths. Consequently, we would be asked to think not only about
what our texts argued, but also about how they were constructed.
These documents would be projected on a screen and "presented"
to the class at various points throughout the semester.

Because of the combination of texts read in the course (beginning with Gilles Deleuze and Foucault), the amount of writing and presenting required, and the way in which the course
was talked about—there was a great deal at stake in participating in this rigor with "competence." One of the professors of the
course insisted that it would be treated "like a graduate course,"
and though his words may have been intended to acknowledge
the capability and potential of the students, it also made the course

"count" more, made the work seem more important and the possibility of critiquing it somehow riskier. It made fitting into the arena, behaving as a successful participant, even more important. Consequently, I looked to my professors and to my peers to discover the course's "ideal subject"—who we were expected to be as students.

On the second day of class, each of the professors presented his own Storyspace document. One produced a document that analyzed moments in his own educational history, drawing visible (and metaphoric) links between Foucault's discussion of the panopticon and the educational practices he experienced as a student through a layered text of prose and poetry. The other professor, however, presented a very linear (also "theoretical" and "dense") document that simply used the boxes to divide paragraphs, all the while joking that he couldn't quite get the hang of this "transgressive writing." While this moment could be read as a teacher demonstrating his own learning in process, as he was struggling to work against the traditions in which he was educated, it seemed to serve instead as an ongoing joke in our class. We all knew these nonlinear texts didn't count as much as other texts, and his "difficulty" with them gave him license not to have to engage them. Since he already demonstrated mastery in the genre that was culturally valued—the genre of most of the published texts we read during the semester—his inability to deal with the poetic, the nonlinear or transgressive text, could be laughed off. He would simply turn those "poetic" texts over to the other professor. So while this disruption of form was encouraged, it was at the same time implicitly dismissed. It wasn't as serious or as rigorous as "real" academic prose.

This was only reinforced when the professors requested that Matt,[3] a student whom many of us knew to be adept at working with theoretical discourses, be the first student to present his Storyspace document, while the rest of us signed up for presentation dates. Matt came to class that second week and projected on the screen a hypertext twenty pages long; the sheer size of his document became the focus among students. His level of performance, combined with his ability to make use of theoretical language that seemed not only difficult but also alienating, set up a "model" with which many would attempt to compete. Many students read this text (and this student) as an ideal intellectual product, engaging with the "right" kinds of knowledges and in the "right" ways. Because we knew he was "chosen," we easily read his text as "correct" and thus "legitimate." While this reading of Matt was not likely intended by the professors, I'm not sure that we knew how to read their choice as anything but a model. We had been learning our whole educational lives to read the teacher's presentation as the model to be mastered and/or imitated.

As I reread my learning narrative as a teacher who has done both—required students to make their writing public and invited a student I perceived to be confident, even "advanced," to get things started—I want to insist that these practices are not inherently problematic. And yet, I wonder, how do students experience my choices? Gore reminds us that no practice is inherently liberating or oppressive. Certainly we name them that way: portfolios are "good," sitting in a circle is "good," lecturing is "bad." But practices never function devoid of specific contexts. It is the interplay of practices and contexts that requires ongoing reflection, consideration.

Because many of us had participated in other classrooms together, Matt had already been marked and named in particular ways by teachers and students alike as a very "rigorous" theorist, doing "dense" and "complex" work. In other words, the stories told about Matt before and during the class were as important in our reading of his work as was his text itself. Given our "knowledge" of Matt, it wasn't surprising that most of us read him as the subject we were supposed to imitate, or his texts as the proper mode of engaging the course content. Consequently, a linear, abstract, somewhat alienating text set the tenor for the rest of the semester. This moment also set up a particular standard for student performance. The writing we shared was to be a finished, polished, theoretically astute product, not a way to begin a dialogue or to collaboratively share in an ongoing writing process with other students. The student and his or her writing would simply assume the role the teacher usually does—performing and presenting a seemingly "finished" knowledge. So this was read not only as a "correct" model for a particular kind of text, but also for a particular kind of performance or mode of being in the classroom.

As a teacher, it is easy for me to forget that the power dynamic in the classroom doesn't exist solely between teacher and students. It exists among students, as well. I think of Julie, an intelligent and soft-spoken young woman in my class, who shared that she feels intimidated by the others, as if they know more than she, have more to contribute than she. Relying on group work is often assumed to "level" out the classroom, to show students that their contributions are valuable, and that their responses are as important as the teacher's. But this assumption risks masking the ways in which dynamics of authority and discipline function even within student groups. It relies on the model of power as property, forgetting the ways it is exercised by subjects (Luke and Gore 1992; Gore 1993; Orner 1992). I must continue to ask: what is overlooked when I assume that my practices function in the name of student empowerment? How do students experience my aims, my pedagogies?

As I remember the course now, I think of it as being made up predominantly of men, although this certainly wasn't the case. Women constituted half of the class; they just rarely spoke. In sharp contrast, many of the male students quickly created a space in which they joked, debated, and steered the social and theoretical agenda. My primary mode of participation in this classroom—which foregrounded the sharing of student voices—was, ironically, silence. But it wasn't only the women who were silent. Another male student—highly regarded for his "intellect"—spoke surprisingly little throughout the class. Unlike many of the women, however, his body and the discourse surrounding him spoke louder than his silence. He seemed to come prepared to speak every day, and, in fact, brought supplementary texts to prove it. Stacked in front of him on his desk was a pile of books—and not just any books—books written by those whose articles we were discussing that day, books that were related to our topic of conversation, books written by Authors whose names spoke for themselves. The books were his armor—a literal demonstration that he had already "acquired" the right knowledge—and they made his silence not invisible but penetrating. As Mimi Orner argues, silence cannot be read in any one way or as the result of any single cause. "There may be compelling conscious and unconscious reasons for not speaking—or for speaking, perhaps more loudly, with silence" (1992, 81). This student's silence was not read as a lack—as I felt mine to be—but a presence. People wondered what lurked behind his silence. On the contrary, the silence of the women was not spoken about and seemed to simply go unnoticed. Among all those "student voices," it remained unheard.

Silence plagued my years as a student—my years, that is, in "student-centered" classrooms. For most of my education, I was rewarded for my silence, my goodness, my obedience. And then the rules changed: good behavior meant speaking, contributing, participating. But I knew the rules had not gone away: there were still "correct" contributions, there were still valued ways of speaking. I remained silent as I tried to figure out what mode of speech would lead to acceptance, legitimacy.

Now, as a teacher, I am one of those who value, sometimes even beg for, participation. I am happiest on the days the classroom is filled with noise, with students jumping to give voice to their opinions, ideas. Perhaps I want to give my students the experience I wish I had had earlier; I want them to feel entitled to speak. I want to empower them. And yet in many of my classes, too, some of the brightest women remain silent. I talk to them about it, I ask students to tell me what would better enable them to participate, I work to adapt my pedagogy to better enable more students to speak.

Orner reminds me, though, that "liberatory" educators must do more: we must ask ourselves why we want students to speak. "[We] must continually examine our assumptions about our own positions, those of our students, the meanings and uses of student voice, our power to call for students to speak, and our often unexamined power to legitimate and perpetuate unjust relations in the name of student empowerment" (77). Even more, she argues that we must not label silence in any single way: as resistance, as internalized oppression, as false consciousness.

I look back on my student silence and know it was complicated. I wonder, how can I know what informs my own students' silences? How can I respond to the unknowable? Maybe this is a better question: Why do I want my students to speak? And to consider this: Why was it so important for me to speak?

My frustration reached a peak during the several weeks we spent reading Foucault's *Discipline and Punish*, the level of conversation remaining abstract, as my awareness of the power relations acting to silence the women grew stronger. As a result of grappling with this text, I began to understand my own self-monitoring in new ways, noting the ways I controlled my own ideas and language. Each time I wanted to speak I interrogated myself, determining whether my comment would be deemed relevant to the current discussion. But we discussed disciplinary tactics abstractly, as if they existed only in a culture outside of the classroom. Despite the curriculum's claim to focus on daily life, here "theory" and "culture" were defined such that speaking from lived experience seemed directly antithetical to the "rigor" required of the class. Our study of culture excluded the culture of the classroom in which we were learning. Rather than risk seeming intellectually deficient, then, many of the women simply remained silent—leaving our astute readings of the gender dynamics we experienced for post-class conversation.

This reading, of course, came later. It came when I was asked to study this moment as a graduate student, to make sense of it given my new theoretical knowledge of critical and feminist pedagogy. It came, in other words, through ongoing dialogue with this moment, which allowed me to see myself as student through a new lens. At the time, I understood the gap between what was "supposed" to happen and what I was experiencing to work on two levels: a social level, which was tied to power dynamics that resulted from gendered positions; and an individual level, which often led me to blame myself for my (seeming) inability to speak. Though neither was, in and of itself, sufficient, the former enabled me—and other women—to begin to act. It allowed us to see the classroom as a text that could be read, critiqued, and even revised (Lee 2000).

Talking with other women outside the class allowed us to begin to understand how we were being excluded from the pedagogy; this was key, since it became easy to simply blame ourselves. Interrupting the discourse itself, however, remained extremely difficult. In an attempt to do so, another female student, Tracy, and I worked outside of class to examine the contexts surrounding our silence and to consider possibilities for interrupting it. Interested in finding ways to make use of Foucault's work for our own project—rather than demonstrating our mastery of it or solely critiquing it—we worked to engage this text, to show how it enabled us to re-see culture. In doing so, we prepared a Storyspace document examining women's internalization of the panopticon and its effects on the female body. Shaping the boxes of our story space in a corset—perhaps a metaphor for how we ourselves felt in the class (small, contained, restricted)—we wove together feminist theory, narrative, and popular discourse as a means of revealing the disciplining of women's sexuality, reproductive organs, and (excess) flesh. We had much at stake in this project, as we hoped that projecting our multilayered text, which made use of and challenged Foucault, would serve both to interrupt the trajectory of the class and allow us a space to speak. Unfortunately, on the day we were to speak, to intervene, the presentations were overscheduled and we ran out of time before our turn came. Perhaps Magda Gere Lewis says it best: "While the experience of being consciously, deliberately, and overtly dismissed is painful, the experience of being invisible is brutalizing" (1993, 137).

Though this was not the outcome for which Tracy and I hoped, I read this moment now—this development of a project— as one of possibility. I am reminded, as a teacher, of the learning that occurs in unexpected and unplanned ways, sometimes in a response to the troubling dynamics I would rather remove entirely from my classroom. It was at this moment that Tracy and I assumed responsibility for the class dynamic, interrupted it, claimed ownership of it. Should we have had to? I still wonder. But as I see it now, developing that project was a way to insist that other voices needed to be heard. Maybe it shows, even, that something about the pedagogy was working. It's just that critical pedagogy does not work as neatly as promised, where the teacher turns over authority, the students assume it, and the class is liberated. Many teacher-scholars have pointed out the struggle teachers undergo as they seek to enact critical pedagogy (Orner 1992;

Ellsworth 1989; Payne1994); here I am reminded of the struggle that students are also asked to undertake.

At the same time, I wonder about the responsibility of the critical teacher. Can authority ever really be "turned over"? And can't teacher authority be used for productive ends?

I left the room in tears—an ultimate embarrassment in such a space. We later received an apology from our instructors, and a "Why didn't you speak up?" from a few of the male students when we later complained to them, but we never did present our document in the classroom that semester.

The question of speaking up is an interesting one, of course, because underlying it is the assumption that we were positioned equally in the classroom, all of us feeling equally entitled to freely enter and disrupt the direction of the course. As well, framing the question in terms of "you" places the responsibility on the individual not speaking—relieving all those contributing to the dynamic from having to examine their own complicity. This is a consequence, I would contend, of the assumption that a critical classroom is inherently a democratic space in which power is shared, which exists somehow outside of the social order being critiqued.

Here, we failed to consider how speech acts are contextually based and dependent upon how power relations are manifest in the local site in which they are engaged (as well as how speech acts reflect and create power relations). Though Orner argues that it seems "impossibly naïve" to think there can be a genuine "sharing of voices" in the classroom, what does seem possible, she argues, "is an attempt to recognize the power differentials present and to understand how they impinge upon what is sayable and doable in that specific context" (1992, 81). So rather than questioning individual women about their silence, the question that needed to be asked was "Why aren't the women speaking?" This question puts the attention where it belongs—not on the individual but on the contexts informing who listens and who speaks, who is allowed comfort and who is not.

How much can the teacher control these contexts? What is his or her responsibility?

Because there was much at stake in speaking within this particular discourse, our document emerged from a contradictory location; we wanted both to disrupt the course, and at the same time to be sanctioned by it. When our professors read the document, we received a great deal of praise not only for the "content" but also for the "transgressive" ways in which we'd made use of the technology. They regretted, they told us, that it had not entered the classroom so that other students could see the possibilities of Storyspace. While there is no question that Tracy and I felt a certain pleasure from the approval stamped on our work, this approval had to be negotiated with our feelings of "lack" in the classroom. The driving force behind our work was a shared desire to bring about different discussion in the classroom and to make public our ideas; the fact that we were later praised for work that wasn't allowed to enter the classroom space made us question the place of feminist critique and whether its acceptance was contingent upon its containment.

Around the same time Tracy and I were attempting to interrupt the course dynamics with our writing project, another female student (one who spoke often in seemingly comfortable ways) attempted to do the same through a public e-mail sent to the class distribution list. She explained that after speaking with another member of the class who felt her comments were being devalued, she felt compelled to "call" people on their classroom behavior and elitism. She made clear that she was "watching" people's responses to others' comments and that those who called themselves "theory boys/girls" had better rethink their actions. Her message quite literally added another "gaze" to the complex ways in which spectatorship and surveillance were already at work in the classroom. In response to it, I received several phone calls that night—from both male and female students—asking, "Who do you think she means?" and "Do you think she means me?" While her message evoked a certain level of fear among her classmates, it made the subtle relations in the class crystal-clear.

On the one hand, the student's e-mail message could be seen to signify the "success" of a critical pedagogy. Students, after all, are "to discipline themselves in the critical or democratic classroom, relying on each other rather than the teacher" (Gore 1993, 115). As I look back as a teacher, I am struck by the degree to which this student felt entitlement to read this classroom, to change it, to act as an authority. The message serves as a clear

*demonstration that students had learned to regulate one another—
to "make choices, organize, and act on their own beliefs" (Giroux
1988b, 69). But this, of course, does not guarantee that the dynamics were any more liberating than when the teacher occupied
the central position of authority. In fact, it seems we had learned
to regulate one another in ways that perpetuated unproductive
and intellectually harmful dynamics, allowing those who already
felt entitled to speak to serve a judiciary and policing role.*

The e-mail message remained on e-mail—no one, students or
professors, mentioned it inside the course. Though it was intended
as a "public" act—and indeed, had public effects—it was left to
be internalized privately. Because this message wasn't engaged, it
only reinforced the notion that discussion about the class was
best left outside, or at least, was less important than the content
we engaged. Bringing the text of the e-mail into the conversation
of the course—as painful and risky as that may have been—might
have enabled us to talk about the way in which power was being
exercised, how we understood terms like "theory boy," the goals
of the course, and the ways in which silence was being read.

*It is a big request I make of my teachers. I am asking them to
make the course a text in itself to be read and critiqued by the
students. As much as it seems a sort of "natural" request to be
making of a "critical" classroom, I think of what doing so would
have meant: the professors would have had to "give up" their
agenda, in order to make their pedagogy—its successes and fail-
ings—visible; they would have had to make room for the unpre-
dictable, the range of emotional responses students were
experiencing; and we all would have had to live in discomfort, as
we shared our very different experiences of the course.*

While the dynamics of the course remained consistent until
its end, I would argue that the real critical and collaborative work
began after the course—an occurrence that certainly disrupts the
notion that courses exist within the institutionally sanctioned time
and space of semesters and classrooms. Many of us began our
own conversations with each other and with the professors, reflecting on what happened, and why and how. The instructors
spoke of the difficulty of collaborative teaching, the students of
the level of performance required and the experience of discomfort and competition. For me, then, the real work began when

we started exploring the pedagogy of the course—the way in which "knowledges" were transmitted—rather than assuming that pedagogy was simply a neutral process marginal to the course's content.

Fortunately, the opportunity to publicly discuss the course came when our professors asked for volunteers to speak at a small sociology conference to be held at our campus that summer. Although the panel was intended to discuss the use of Storyspace in our classroom site, the "intent" was interrupted when one of the female students, who had remained silent throughout almost the entire course of the semester, began her presentation saying, "It's strange that I'm here now presenting on this course since I rarely spoke in class." Her disruption opened a space in the conversation which allowed for an examination of the levels of performance expected in the course, and how the Storyspace served as a means to "display" the work we'd done rather than to share and produce knowledge collectively as a result of one another's readings of the texts. Most important, she shifted the conversation in a way that insisted we consider the lived experience of those who are "written on" by a pedagogy, demonstrating that the pedagogy must be read as its own "rhetoric of knowledge" and that silence served as its own "text" in the classroom, which itself needed to be questioned and problematized.

While it's interesting to consider what allowed for this interruption—perhaps including the post-course conversations and the attentive audience of mainly female teachers—it is also necessary to consider what might have facilitated such reflexive practices in the classroom itself. How could the silence of the women in that classroom have been used in transformative ways—allowing us to learn from it and disrupt the conditions that gave rise to it? Gore suggests that "if pedagogy is not just received by students, but is 'unpacked' with students, the work of unpacking will occur at least partly 'outside the regime [of truth]'" (1993, 143). With this in mind, allowing room for the kind of work that was ultimately done outside of class during the course itself might have opened possibilities for momentarily getting "outside" to interrogate and critique what was going on within.

I have told this story many times, and at different moments gleaned different lessons, understandings, questions from it: make the pedagogy a central text in the class; examine how silence speaks; consider the way gender informs the classroom; keep an eye on the contradictions between pedagogical ideals and practices. But coming to these conclusions, rendering the story so as to finally finish it, contain it, has never been the most fruitful part of the process. Indeed, the more I return to it, bring my current experiences, questions, confusions as a teacher to bear on it, the more I realize that I *can't* finish it, and if there is a lesson to be learned, it is not to stop returning. It is to continue to place it in dialogue with my current teaching practices.

Teacher Learning as Disorientation

I conclude this chapter with one more learner story, written from my perspective as a teacher. I do so to offer another challenge to the notion that teachers can finally be trained, but even more, to show that it is the process of questioning and reflecting that offers possibility for change. I have chosen this particular story for two central reasons: it parallels, on several levels, my student story, raising issues of silence and speech, power differentials, and discomfort, and it demonstrates my desire, as a teacher, to be in control, trained, oriented. At the same time, it reminds me that those moments when things unravel are often the moments when the best opportunities for revision occur. I am still learning from this story.

From Teacher to Student: Still Learning

It's my first semester teaching at a small Jesuit university in the Midwest. I've chosen a novel, *Push,* as one of the central texts in my first-year writing course.[4] It makes perfect sense: it will open the eyes of this largely homogeneous student population, and it will allow us to engage issues of literacy, poverty, and race, as well as to study the powerful way in which Sapphire has composed this text. It will allow us a way to connect to the marginalized; this, after all, is part of our university's mission.

And it makes no sense: it will make students feel uncomfortable, alienated; they won't be able to relate; it might reinforce their stereotypes; it will offend, push. I worry about the students reading the text over Thanksgiving break. I imagine angry calls from parents, if they catch a glimpse of the "foul" (as several of my students name it) language in the book.

But, I think, this is *important*. Anyway, one hurdle at a time. I think, if I can just predict them, perhaps we can glide, rather than trip, over them. I want to be in control.

Hurdle 1: Black English

Getting over it: I want students to see Sapphire's choice to compose in Black English as a crucial and legitimate one; I want them to see Black English as a language.

Reading: an essay by James Baldwin and one by June Jordan, both discussing the politics and history of Black English.

Writing: a letter in which you write as either Baldwin or Jordan to E. D. Hirsch, discussing his definition of "Standard English."

Let's begin with what you wrote for today. Silence. I wonder if they've read or written. Several trail in late, ten, twelve, fourteen minutes late. I control my anger, casting disapproving glances their way. I ask again. Katie and Angie point out how they refuted various aspects of Hirsch's argument by challenging it with historical or anecdotal evidence from Baldwin and June's argument. *Good*, I think, *Good*. Things are going as planned.

And then:

I found so many gaps in Baldwin's argument that I wrote my letter to Hirsh without any support; that seems to be his style, Jake said. *But wasn't the point to compose a rhetorically effective text, to fairly represent Baldwin's point?* I ask. After all, I think, we were certainly careful to "listen" to Hirsch.

I guess, he shrugs. *I thought Baldwin just seemed really angry, so in my letter, Baldwin made Hirsch look like an idiot,* Mike says.

Where is Baldwin angry? How does a seemingly "angry" voice function in the piece? What cultural reasons does he point to that might fuel his anger? Silence. Silence. Silence.

And yet, maybe I am asking for silence. I don't want to hear their anger at the novel, at Jordan, at Baldwin.

After sitting through more than enough silence, I end class early, announcing that I am disappointed with the level of engagement. (I hate assuming the role of the "disappointed teacher." But I am disappointed.) *Anyway,* I add, *this will give me time to speak briefly with each one of you about your last portfolios.*

Shauna, the only African American woman in the class, approaches me for her portfolio. I ask her why she has been so quiet. I know she likes the novel, and she told me earlier that she was excited to discuss Black English. *I wanted to speak,* she replies, *but I was so angry that I couldn't. I just can't believe what they say sometimes.*

I worry about the position she is being asked to occupy—the one black woman in a white class. I tell her as much.

No, she says, *I'm glad we're reading it. I'm used to this.* I ask her to come to my office hours, so we can talk more.

(She agrees. She does not come.)

After most of the students have filtered out, Kerri and Anna approach me. *I think we know why people were so quiet today,* they say. *Shauna just keeps making faces when people make comments. No one wants to say anything because it seems like she's so mad. She's making it hard to talk.*

I am disgusted: white students blaming the single black student for silencing them, blaming her anger for their discomfort. But I can't say this. *Thanks for letting me know. You know, I think it must be hard to be the only black person in the room— that's a lot of pressure to bear. I need to think about how we can make it a better climate for everyone to participate in these discussions,* I say. *But really, thanks for telling me.*

For the next class, I prepare a speech. Practice it, even. I want desperately to feel in control, to demonstrate confidence and certainty. I acknowledge that I had been (at least partly) wrong the period before. I hadn't thought about how hard it is to discuss race. I say I knew that acknowledging this might not make it easier, it wasn't a solution. But I want to put it out there all the same. I share with them that as an undergraduate student, a good girl, a good student, I, too, had worried most of all about offending students of color with my comments. *(See, I relate to you.)*

This was true even after hearing from several of my African American classmates that it is much worse not to engage these issues, to repress them, to pretend them away. A couple of students confirm that this is exactly how they feel—afraid of offending others. Some seem to look relieved.

Shauna is absent that day. She'd written to tell me that her sister had gone into labor, and she needed to be with her. *But isn't my speech trying to smooth things over for the white students?* I want to make space for Shauna to speak; I want to make space for the novel to speak. And yet, I can't stop worrying about the offended white students.

A few days later, Shauna sends me an e-mail:

Sorry it took me so long to get back to you. My sister did not have her baby it was false alarm (I guess). I just have a quick question to ask you because I am reading some of my peers' essays (which I find rather disturbing) and I really need to know something. When I was not in class were people more willing to talk about the book?

I don't want to answer her question.

Shauna: I made sure to raise the issue in our discussion on the 22nd about the difficulty—in general—of talking about race. So we talked a bit about it then, and more about it during the last class. I was really sorry you couldn't be there. I'm more than happy to talk with you further about this, and about the essays you're reading. Can you come by during my office hours? SS

I don't want to answer her question.

Dr. S.: I can understand you raising the awareness on the "difficulty" of discussing race, but my question is did more people talk and was the discussion free-flowing and not dead (so to speak) as it was when I was in class?

I don't want to answer her question. She knows it.

Shauna and I meet outside of class. She has drafts of her peers' essays with her, one of which she found disturbing, condescending to black women. She reads me the response she's written to the essay: it is bold and clear. It is not rude, but it is not cloaked, either, in polite, sugar-coated language. She shares that she has been silent in class because of her anger, but also because she has been afraid to speak in class for fear of generating conflict, which she doesn't like.

I begin to wonder if the "respectful" dynamics in class that I encouraged all semester weren't having a negative effect. Politeness, respect, lack of emotion—at what cost? I encourage her—despite my nagging fear that this might upset the white student (for whom is my pedagogy?)—to share her peer review. I encourage her to share her ideas with the class. As she pointed out, "We deal with race every day. Why are we so bad at talking about it?"

The next day, Shauna breaks her long silence, telling her classmates that she can't understand why they were having such a problem with the novel, that their responses seem, well, "stupid," to her. It is an important book, she tells them, one that touches on the reality of many. To her, it doesn't seem so strange. And yet, we keep talking about how hard it is for *us* to read it. What about those whose lives are affected by poverty, racism, abuse?

Jake responds in a calm, measured voice, relying on words that sound suspiciously familiar. They come from the syllabus. He argues that her calling the other students stupid is violating the kind of respect we are supposed to demonstrate to each other in the class. His becomes the voice of authority and discipline, using the rhetoric of the teacher to enforce his position.

I quickly agree with Jake that respect is indeed important (though I do not call him on his own lack of respect), and then work to steer the conversation back to Shauna's point, to help the students hear it even through the anger they resent. I wonder if I am losing something in my calm, "rational" translation of her words.

(I remember this day as a failure, but when I look to my teaching journal entry from that day, I find this: *Kaitlin made comment that she felt uncomfortable—probably we all do, but that's good. Molly remarked that this exactly the conversation Sapphire would want us to have, that the book begs of us.* They remind me that I do not need to, that I cannot, protect them from discomfort; they remind me that discomfort can be productive.)

Toward the end of the semester, students begin to find ways of sharing with me, in private, their feelings about the novel. They are given the option, as part of their final project, to write about whether, and under what conditions, this novel should be taught. In class, many students argue that students should not be forced to read it, to encounter the graphic reality it details. But the students who approach me privately have something else to say. Mike tells me that students at our private university, more than anywhere else, need to read the book. He felt he couldn't say this in class, however, or he would get too angry. (This would be bad, he insists.) I wonder what we lost because of silence, because of the rule that we should not get angry in class.

Beth tells me she wasn't at all shocked by the book; she was more shocked by the responses of her fellow students. *I overheard some students saying in another class that they'd never seen a black person before,* she said. *It's like this school is Disneyland, and they don't want their day rained on. The book is like a bad ride.* I ask her if I should teach it the next semester. *Oh yeah,* she says. *Teach it first.*

I don't teach this book for four years.

When I do, I am faced with an eerily familiar situation: a class with only one African American student, a slow-moving discussion, despite many claims that "I didn't want to stop reading." One student shares that she finds it difficult to believe, and disturbing, that no one looked into the pregnancy of a twelve-year-old girl by her father. "Oh, I'm not surprised," Kenisha interjects. "This is Harlem. They've got far more patients than the doctors can take care of, and they'd probably need to be looking into all of their lives. The nurse probably knew that the best she could do was to be kind to Precious. I've been places like this, I know people like Precious." But then Kenisha interrupts herself to say that her mind is spinning. She puts her head in her hands. *I've got so much to say.* She pauses, "I just don't want to offend anyone."

I feel the knot in my stomach rise to my throat. This book insists on making a mess. My teaching requires me to surrender to the mess—a mess that means people might get offended, students might be mad at me, racist comments might be made. But this time I decide that if I can help it, the one African American student in the room will not be silenced. I want to use my authority differently this time. I gently nudge her later in the conversation, "Kenisha, you said you had a lot of thoughts spinning. Anything you'd like to share?"

She says it again. "I just don't want to offend anyone."

And so we talk about it: offending people. How hard it is to have these conversations at this institution. How afraid the white students feel of sounding ignorant at best, racist at worst. "But how do we get beyond this—beyond talking about how difficult it is to discuss these issues?" Silence ensues. Jenny says that the point of education is to have these conversations, and suggests that maybe we need to think about how our education has failed us if we aren't able to discuss something like *Push*. A few people nod. More silence.

As Kenisha packs her bag to leave, I ask her, quietly, if she's OK. She tells me that she loves the book, but it's too familiar. She knows Precious in too many variations. She is angry that so many people are ignorant of situations like that of Precious. She is angry about the two lives she leads: at home and at our university. About the parts of her she must leave behind as she steps onto our well-manicured campus. *This is the first time,* she says, *that I need to bring my other life into the classroom, because they need to know that these stories are real. If they hear them from me,* she wagers, *they might get it.* I assure her that she doesn't have to. Those stories are hers. *I have to do it for me,* she points at her chest. But she worries about what will happen when they leave the classroom. Will she become one of "them"? Will she become invisible?

We don't know what will happen. But we are committed to the higher risk, in hope of a higher yield.

(Un)endings: Unraveling and Renewal

In an earlier draft of this conclusion, I offered evidence of both positive and negative results of these moments. But this move only reinforces the notion that pedagogical outcomes can be neatly categorized into "good" and "bad." I agree with Elizabeth Boquet, who argues that "good" and "bad" are labels that "belie the complexity of the work of teaching and learning and writing and being human" (2002, 148). Instead, I want to embrace the complex effects (those that I can name—many are beyond my knowledge, I'm sure) of this moment.

While the above stories may demonstrate greater dissonance than we experience on a daily basis, they are not exceptional in their complexity. Pedagogical moments are always complex; the teaching process is filled with what Brunner calls "breaks" and "ruptures." Rather than preparing teachers to go to work when they encounter such moments, to mend them quickly and efficiently with institutional authority, knowledge, or practices, we would do better to help them learn to embrace the "unraveling" (1994, 39). Brunner argues that it is only through unraveling, reflection, and rethinking that we might reach "a state of renewal," that we might see in a new light (39). And that, to me, is what teacher development is about—breaks, ruptures, unraveling, and renewal.

One reviewer of this manuscript suggested that she or he needed to know more about *what* learning took place and *how* it occurred so that the story wouldn't "just keep repeating itself under the same circumstance forever." I can point to some of the vehicles for the learning that took place: reflection on these moments with other teachers and students; writing about them so as to examine them from different perspectives and angles; and placing them in dialogue with other classes and texts. But I can't so easily boil the learning down to simple lessons (e.g., don't teach controversial texts at a mostly white school, or make sure to have a conversation about discussing race before actually doing so). I don't doubt that for as long as I work to engage issues of race in my classroom, certain complexities will repeat themselves—albeit in different forms and as a result of different dynamics. As long as I teach a mostly white population, it is likely that the often single student of color in my class will bear particular pressures. But I have decided that we must discuss race, and so I can't avoid the inevitable rupture that results. And I can't apply a premade solution that will guarantee a stress-free dialogue. What I can do is to make use of the rupture—to see it as a possibility to work from rather than a problem to squelch. Only then might it lead to renewal.

In discussing tutor training for writing centers, Boquet notes that most new tutors (like new teachers) would appreciate a "shield of strategies" to protect them from anxiety, uncertainty, and dissonance (77). This, however, would only be a false shield, which would not only fail to "fix" all difficult moments, but might protect them from the productivity and possibility inherent in these interactions. Relying on music metaphors of feedback and distortion, Boquet contends that we need to develop a "greater tolerance of distortion," a recognition that there "exists an element of distortion at play in every interchange" (75). She pushes toward a "higher-risk/higher-yield" model for writing center work. One of the tutors in Boquet's book notes, "If I had had [a handbook or template on tutoring] I would have felt secure. The summer session has taught me that you have to be invested, have to hear [the students], have to hear what they need from you, what you can offer them. It gives you a lot of freedom" (101).

Her arguments, I believe, resonate in the writing classroom and in teacher-preparation sites, as well. We need not only to offer new teachers a "shield" of effective practices that will help them feel a sense of affective confidence, but also to help them gain comfort with discomfort—to see their questions not as a sign of a deficit, but as a strength. This is not to downplay the importance of teachers and tutors' need for confidence (a need certainly highlighted in my narrative); instead, it is to suggest that one way to help new teachers gain confidence is to enable them to view moments of tension and dissonance as laden with possibility. As Tremmel points out, we've already done well to encourage academic preparation and best practices in teacher-training sites. What we haven't done adequately is to create possibilities for ongoing reflection and learning: for making use of the complicated and disorienting moments that are inevitable in teaching—for new and experienced teachers alike.

In the next chapter I will continue to argue that teacher development is best enabled, and confidence most productively built, in sites where ongoing questioning and learning is supported and valued. There I will argue for, and offer examples of, a collaborative teacher community designed to promote pedagogical praxis and inquiry.

The Teacher as Owner

Teacher Visits: Three Short Stories

Story 1

My first semester of teaching was a roller-coaster ride. One moment I was thrilled at my own good luck to be earning money, however little, to work with bright, interesting writers. The next, I was overwhelmed by all that the job entailed, particularly as I confronted twists and turns for which I felt perpetually unprepared.

I was especially uneasy, then, when I received repeated e-mail messages from Amy, the writing director, asking when she could visit my class. I tried ignoring, stalling, and finally explaining to her that I did not yet feel ready to open my class to someone else (let alone my "boss"). Just give me some more time, I pleaded. But she was persistent. She wanted to come, and to come this semester, in the next few weeks.

Your nervousness makes sense, Amy noted, since usually classroom visits are evaluative. But this visit is not intended as a surveillance mechanism, she promised. *I see it as an opportunity for me to learn from you.*

I didn't believe her; I couldn't imagine the visit as anything other than evaluative. I was the new teacher; she was the experienced teacher, and the program director. And it was for this reason (her authority) that I finally agreed to the visit. We set a time and date.

When she came to my class, I was surprised that she joined the circle of students, rather than sitting in the back corner as "the observer." She also joined the conversation, asking questions and offering her own perspectives on the issues at hand. In many ways, she was more of a participant than an observer, which eased my anxiety considerably.

Even so, I was nervous to hear Amy's assessment of my teaching and asked that we meet to discuss the class right away. I couldn't shake the notion that this was an evaluation of my teaching. Amy said she had planned to take some time to reflect, but sensing my anxiety, she agreed to sit down for a conversation immediately. She began by describing what she learned from my teaching—how it enabled her to rethink some of her own pedagogical choices. For instance, observing the way I allowed silence in the discussion helped Amy to think about how quickly she rushed to fill silence in her own classroom—often, she said, with her own voice.

She also helped me see aspects of my teaching that were previously invisible to me. For instance, during the class's large-group workshop, I often cut myself off too quickly in order to turn discussion back to the students. I explained that I wanted to enact a "student-centered" classroom, and I believed—though I had never before articulated this notion—that this meant I should talk as little as possible. I wanted to be careful not to take up too much space, to make my comments central. We begin to tease out this issue, exploring the limits and possibilities of our conceptions of "student-centered" pedagogy. The discussion, then, moved from the specific site of my classroom to a larger pedagogical issue in which both Amy and I had a stake.

Story 2

It was our first Writing Sequence meeting of the semester. With a year of teaching under my belt, I was serving as assistant director of the program, and Amy and I had generated some ideas for the year—practices that we hoped would enable teaching community and allow opportunities for us to learn from each other. In addition to the regular teacher meetings, Amy suggested that we also establish classroom visits, beginning as soon as the first two weeks of class. It was important, she insisted, to normalize them as a regular part of teaching.

The new teachers expressed anxiety. In fact, they almost immediately rejected the idea. I can't say that I was surprised, but I was disappointed, since I had come to believe that visits could function as collaborative learning moments. Finally, after much discussion, one teacher, Anna, introduced a compromise, agreeing to the visits, but insisting that she would need at least one month before anyone visited. Amy was troubled by this, asking why Anna felt that she would need to first learn on her own, without the input of other teachers. This, she said, was the very idea we were working to disrupt—that our teaching practices are somehow private, something we develop in isolated classrooms, with the door closed.

But Anna insisted, again, that she wouldn't be ready to open up her classroom to another teacher so early in the term, that it would take time for us to trust one another enough to share the texts of our teaching. And then she issued this reminder: *You can't enforce teaching community.*

Story 3

It was my second year as an assistant professor and director of composition. I was in charge of administering a first-year writing program whose twenty sections were taught mainly by veteran part-time instructors. Knowing I could learn as much (or more) from them as they could from me, I was anxious to begin to create opportunities to build teaching community. I established monthly "composition conversations," often led by part-time instructors; I created occasions to discuss the curriculum, so that I could learn from them about how it was enacted; I initiated a May workshop for assignment sharing and syllabus development. But classroom visits were another matter. University policy spoke louder than my good intentions; every part-time instructor was required to be observed once a year by a full-time faculty member. *Full-time faculty members, however, were not held to the same requirement.*

Still, I thought, these visits needed not be punitive; in fact, they could serve as a site of mutual learning, as I'd experienced them in the past. I tried to explain as much in a composition meeting—one of the rare occasions when all of the part-time and full-time instructors who teach in our core curriculum were gathered. The visits, I told the teachers, are not intended to be evaluative, but an opportunity for mutual teacher learning. They allow me to see the various ways English 150 is conceived and enacted, and provide us an opportunity to discuss the curriculum. I further explained that my required post-visit write-up would take the form of a "learning letter" in which I would describe what transpired and explain what I learned and wondered about during the visit. The letter would not be read by the chair unless the teacher chose to share it. And, I added, I would love to have them visit my classroom, as well. So far, no one has taken me up on this invitation.

The Ethic of Radical Individualism and Classroom Ownership

As each of the above stories demonstrates, opening our classroom doors to one another is a practice we learn to resist for its evaluative implications. We know that visits are often reserved only for those whose employment is tenuous and/or who are still considered learners—TAs, part-time instructors, untenured faculty members. To be visited is to show oneself as something other than a professor—a finished knower who owns his or her classroom. In fact, climbing the professorial ladder typically means acquiring greater classroom autonomy, a sentiment we see in the third story above: full-time faculty are not expected to be evaluated, because of their professorial (professional) status. They are granted "ownership" of their classrooms, and an enforced visit might be considered an invasion of privacy, an intrusion on academic freedom. (This may be why part-time instructors stop by my office or approach me in the hallway to talk about teaching issues, but don't come to my classroom.) At the same time, part-time instructors are merely renters, and therefore the landlords/managers may enter (with "permission," of course) at any time.

Indeed, "academic freedom" is often (mis)used to make the case that each professor has the right to engage the classroom as he or she sees fit; his or her responsibility (as Hart reminds us) begins and ends with himself or herself, with his or her knowledge. This tie between professing and privatization is fueled by what Phelps calls "an ethic of radical individualism," which discourages collaborative learning among teachers, setting up practices such as classroom visits as "intrusions threatening a private space of autonomy, intimacy and power" (1991, 866). Here, private classroom ownership becomes more important than participation in a shared intellectual project. The result is often what James Seitz calls a "disconnected set of monologues" rather than a dialogue in support of a "collectively articulated project" (2002, 162).

In this chapter I will argue that in order to challenge the notion of "professor as owner" and the ethic of radical individualism that informs it, three steps are necessary. First, we are in need of new conceptions of collaborative teacher inquiry. This work involves the formation of teaching communities committed to studying the local contexts in which teaching takes place, the curriculum. In fact, as Phelps argues, the relations of teacher knowledge and practice "can be understood most profoundly in the context of a *teaching community* collectively developing and testing a *curriculum*" (866). Because visions only function within local contexts and through specific practices, the second step is a careful examination of the social and institutional contexts that have contributed to our current state of "radical individualism" in teaching. It requires, in other words, an awareness of what we have taken to be natural, and what we need to work against. Third, we need more discussions of the practices and processes through which teaching communities are built.

Later in the chapter, I will offer familiar practices that are reconceptualized in order to promote community-based teacher and curriculum development. First, however, I will examine the model Phelps poses in the context of current institutional structures that hinder such a vision.

New Conceptions of Community and Curriculum

With Phelps, I want to promote a model of teacher learning that is equally dependent upon community and curriculum. Two assumptions are central to this model: (1) teacher learning is a dialogic process, aided by interaction with teachers and students; and (2) teachers benefit from formalized opportunities to collaboratively inquire into our classrooms, visions, and practices. This inquiry is not intended, however, only to benefit individual teachers or classrooms. Instead, as Phelps notes, "part of the work of the community is to make visible to itself [. . .] the ecology of curricular contexts in which any teaching decision is embedded, not merely abstractly but as vivid, particular realities" (867). As teachers work together to study their classrooms, and to consider how their individual pedagogies contribute to the curriculum, they also create opportunities to study, and potentially revise, the curriculum. According to this model, teacher development and curriculum development go hand in hand. In fact, education theorist Lawrence Stenhouse insists that there is no curricular development without teacher development (1985, 68). If curricula are meaningful, he argues, they serve as expressions of ideas to improve teachers. But I would also argue the opposite. Curricula are served by teacher development, so that as teachers learn from their classroom research and from their work with students, they can ask questions of the curriculum—striving to make it more meaningful for all who participate in it. It is important, then, that we form communities of teachers for whom reflection on local pedagogical sites (and the contexts that shape them) is valued as part of their regular work.

Of course, variations of professorial community have long occupied a central role in academia, even in the research model. Disciplinary knowledge is created and monitored by members of a research community. Michael Polanyi describes scientific communities this way: "scientists administer jointly the advancement and dissemination of science. [. . . They] actually establish the current meaning of the term 'science,' determine what should be accepted as science, and establish the current meaning of the term scientist" (quoted in Phelps 1991, 879). This work, however, in and outside of science, relies as much on exclusion as inclusion, and has tended to leave out those whose work takes place in classrooms. Further, the dynamics informing such communities tends to be agonistic, requiring one to disprove or argue against—rather than build upon—the work that came before one's own (Slevin 1996, 155).

Phelps promotes "practitioner communities," an alternative to the research community, which she distinguishes in two ways. First, while the members of research communities know one another mainly through texts, practitioner communities rely on face-to-face interaction and are concerned primarily with the local sites in which their work takes place. Teacher communities, she argues, focus on "practical knowledge of the institutional setting, the *local* community, and its concrete, materially interdependent activities" (879). But these groups aren't "practical" in the traditional (and derogatory) sense of the term. That is, teachers' work is not limited to reflecting on personal practices and sharing them with one another. Instead, the work of studying one's classroom and community is a mode of intellectual inquiry.

Second, practitioner communities place strong emphasis on local reflexivity—a critical examination of how the community functions, and what effect its practices have on others. As Phelps puts it, "the community needs to study itself: its students, choices and their impacts, structures, conceptual bases, contexts in the university and elsewhere—all more systemically than is possible through reflection alone. Practical inquiry makes the community self-aware, and therefore critical, on the curricular scale" (880).

Though Phelps does not spell out the distinction between "reflexivity" and "reflection," she makes clear that reflection is not sufficient. As Qualley points out, when we reflect, we "fix our thoughts on a subject; we carefully consider it, meditate upon it. [But] self-reflection assumes that individuals can access the contents of their own minds *independently of others*" (1997, 11). Reflexivity, on the other hand, is response "triggered by a dialectical engagement with the other—an other idea, theory, person, culture, text" (11). Practitioner inquiry requires teachers to examine their classrooms "'in view of' the courses taught by other [teachers] preceding and following theirs in the [. . .] curriculum" as well as in relation to "the intellectual experiences of students" (Phelps 1991, 867). This is especially important, because as Phelps points out, through its various modes of practice the community does not just become better aware of the contexts in which it works, but it *creates* them:

> Through its talk, writing, inquiry, and action, members of [a teaching community] are imagining and shaping its writing courses as a developmentally related sequence; translating the university curricula into a particularized range of writing, reading, thinking, and learning tasks set for students; and profiling the stu-

dents themselves as unpredictably diverse and heterogeneous despite their apparent typicalities. Most of all, the program is creating and recreating itself as a social group with some common commitments and understandings. (867)

Though "practitioner" communities share with "research" communities the emphasis on "mutual trust and reciprocal criticism," Phelps ultimately sees them as engaged in different modes of inquiry. As she has it, "practical inquiry refers itself primarily to the work and thought of its own community, and does not take responsibility for its relationship to the disciplinary and interdisciplinary communities at large" (881). By definition, then, practical inquiry—because of the site in which it is engaged—is distinct from disciplinary inquiry.

While Phelps's project seeks ultimately to argue for the richness and complexity of practitioners' work, making it the equivalent of researchers' work, I am not sure the status of the former can be raised without examining the institutional reasons the latter has been privileged. Why is disciplinary work defined as something other than local? As having to do with building abstract knowledge instead of engaging it with students? Even the terms she uses perpetuate a distinction between something called "practice" and something called "theory," one thing known as "teaching" and another as "engaging disciplinary work." My fear is that severing work at the local site from disciplinary conversations risks perpetuating the tendency to reward work for the extent to which it is divorced from the classroom—to credit that which remains on the level of abstraction with disciplinary legitimacy, and consequently, to reduce that which addresses teaching or curricula to "merely practical."

Of course, as the discipline of English has undergone radical changes during the last two decades, many scholars have argued that discussions of the local—particularly concerning English curricula—must and do constitute crucial disciplinary work. In fact, as the field's subject matter has diversified, it has become difficult to avoid curricular questions. What is our object of study or subject matter? What should an English major know or be able to do? What does it mean to teach English? While these questions may still not embody as much value as those deemed more "scholarly" (or abstract), they have received greater attention as answering them has become increasingly important to the discipline. Consequently, a growing number of scholarly texts foreground curricula as a site of intellectual inquiry integral to disciplinary work. Gerald Graff's *Professing Literature* (1987) and Seitz's *Motives for Metaphor: Literacy, Curriculum Reform, and the Teaching of English* (1999) are built out of these very questions. And North's *Refiguring the Ph.D. in English Studies* (2000) examines curricular issues at the doctoral level.

The problem, however, is that even while this "crisis of identity" in English studies has made curricula a site of disciplinary work, it has not tended to result in the kind of teacher communities Phelps promotes, which emphasize "common commitments and understandings" (867). Though the "crisis" has opened a space for discussions across difference, it has more often produced an increased isolation of classrooms within a curriculum, a more deeply ingrained "ethic of radical individualism." Phelps points out, for instance, that despite increasing communal projects and movements, such as writing across the curriculum, classrooms are still often treated as isolated worlds, containing the specialized knowledge of the professor. Worse, the solutions to the problem only seem to further reinforce it. For instance, Graff's oft-cited call to "teach the conflicts" makes the differences or disagreements among individual classrooms the subject of English studies. While this at least functions to make differences visible and public, the emphasis remains on what prevents us from enacting community rather than on what is involved in negotiating and building it. As North sees it, Graff's solution is a "corporate compromise"—a way to hold the "conflicted enterprise together, however loosely, and then—for curricular purposes—[find] some way to present, but at the same time preserve, all its competing interests" (94). Here, professors are allowed to continue to pursue their specialized areas of expertise without considering how their classroom works in dialogue with the professor's classroom across the hall. Consequently, it is easy to perpetuate a dynamic wherein professors are responsible primarily to their own knowledge. And as Seitz points out, as students move between incongruous classrooms, they—not their professors—are left with the burden of "intuit[ing] the larger picture as best they can" (1999, 195).

Because curricula, according to this model, often comprise an eclectic collection of individual courses—the common element being difference and conflict—curricular revision rarely is a community activity. Too often, Seitz insists, teachers imagine possibilities for altering the curriculum by revising their own pedagogy or the contents of their courses. While this is likely to be useful, it is not enough. One composition teacher shifting away from, say, a current-traditional approach or including more theory in his or her course will not alter the systemic problem that has positioned composition as a service course in the first place. As Graff himself argues, the "reduction of education to teaching, which goes hand in hand with the glorification of the autonomous, self-contained course as the natural locus of education, fails to see that educational problems are systemic ones that involve not just individual teaching but the way that teaching is organized" (1990, 831).

Seitz's vision, then, "begins from the hope that teachers of English might yet find a way to work together toward an alternative approach to the teaching of reading and writing" (18). While public debate of differences is one step toward challenging the individualism and isolationism that shapes most curricula, Seitz insists that by resting, finally, on difference, something is lost. This is the "possibility of holding another kind of conversation between courses, one that would envision the differences between teachers, courses and programs not simply as the antagonisms of a discipline in conflict but also as the mutually illuminating forms of inquiry by which English studies investigates the reading and writing of texts" (199). Consequently, Seitz wants to emphasize the potential *alliances* between courses, to discover not only what can be learned from conflict, but also how we can build on what is shared.

If Phelps's vision stops short of seeing teaching communities engaged in testing a curriculum as *disciplinary* work, however, Seitz's stops short of imagining possibilities for building and enacting the teaching communities themselves.[1] What does it mean to create the conditions in which teachers of English can work together across classrooms? Once we have found this shared ground, how do we enact curricula that feature it? And even if we move beyond differences in subject matter, how do we negotiate differences—in institutional location and authority, for instance—

among teachers? While Phelps and Seitz lay important groundwork for teacher community and curriculum development, there remains much work to be done. Because neither teacher community nor curriculum is a product—rather, they are structures that require ongoing examination, reflection, and revision—we need more depictions of how "teacher community collectively developing and testing a curriculum" gets worked out in practice. For this reason, I turn now to several practices aimed at enabling the building (and rebuilding) that such communities require. In each case, I strive to recast practices often associated with enforcing compliance into fostering commitment.

Revisiting Classroom Visits

As I've argued above, the ethic of radical individualism contributes to the notion that the classroom visit is an imposition, a practice designed to make public, and to evaluate and judge, what is assumed to be private. In many ways, the barriers that hinder productive classroom visits parallel those often encountered when we ask students to share their writing—also traditionally assumed to be private—with one another. For many students, the thought of turning over a draft to peers is an anxiety-provoking prospect; they have learned to view sharing their writing—even with each other—as a corrective mechanism, not one intended to further or extend a text. Underlying this assumption is the notion that if they were *better* writers, they would not need feedback from others.

This same belief informs the professorial ideal, where learning is conflated with a lack of authority or mastery. Jordan's 1965 survey of 436 universities and colleges paints one of the clearest pictures of this sentiment. In the survey, nearly one-third of the responders declared "staunchly" that they "never" visited classrooms because, as one respondent said, "Visiting causes students to lose confidence in their teacher" (112). The implicit assumption here is that students should not see their teachers learning as teachers; our classrooms are supposed to be sites where we demonstrate mastery of knowledge, not "drafts" in process. Moreover, the teacher-preparation mechanisms that require opening the classroom door are often considered punitive—a part of the training process deemed unnecessary once one becomes a professor, at which point he or she earns "academic freedom" (i.e., privacy or ownership).

In our writing classes, many of us work to teach students that all writers, no matter their experience levels, benefit from collaborative inquiry into their writing. The same holds true of teaching. I would contend that all teachers, no matter their institutional positions, would benefit from a commitment to collaborative teacher learning, to opening our classroom doors to one another. Within this framework, the classroom visit—what I will dub a *learning* visit—emerges out of *commitment* to mutually agreed-upon goals and considerations, rather than out of *compliance* to top-down visions. These learning visits do not function to evaluate individual teachers, but to enable mutual learning on the parts of both the visited and the visitor.

Of course, declaring a vision of the "learning visit" is not sufficient. As Anna argues in the second story above, teaching community can't be enforced, and entrenched notions of the evaluative visit cannot be simply brushed aside by promises that *this visit will be different*. Instead, the conditions for learning visits must be negotiated within the specific contexts in which they take place, with the participants who engage them. Though these conditions need to be remade every time within each teaching community, I will touch here on several behaviors that I deem key to creating conditions for reciprocity. In describing these behaviors, I will draw from examples of sites where productive conditions for learning visits were established.

Because it is difficult to imagine classroom visits as nonevaluative and mutually enabling, an important first step in establishing such conditions involves *rendering visible participants' assumptions about the purpose of the activity*. How are classroom visits traditionally used in teaching institutions? If you've been visited before, what were the circumstances of the visit? What did the visit enable? What felt restrictive about it? How was the visit indicative of the institutional structure in which it took place? Unpacking the traditional functions of visits—and the way they often serve the entrenched professorial model—not only allows participants to tie individual feelings of anxiety or trepidation to institutional structures, but it also allows them to begin to critique the normative model.

For instance, in a teaching practicum in which I was a student, we began the classroom visit process by articulating and examining the anxiety many of us experienced. A shared fear was that we might be exposed as "frauds," not living up to our pedagogical visions and thus seeming to be "bad" teachers. As we teased out our conflation of learning with fraudulence, we began to see our responses as symptomatic of a model that (falsely) promotes finished or master teachers. Making visible this model allowed us to challenge it: Why is teaching so often privatized? Why do we see teacher learning as something with which we should be somehow finished? Why are we so quick to assume that we learn teaching best on our own, and that it is not a social process? Why do we have so few models of collaborative teacher learning at the university level? But it was not enough to raise these questions once. Because the research model is so deeply entrenched and naturalized, it was important that we keep rendering it visible, so that we could see what we were striving to challenge.

Also key to making visits true learning encounters is *establishing shared goals for and conceptions of the visit*. Rather than enacting a master-apprentice dynamic whereby the visiting teacher comes to evaluate the course using his or her own (often invisible) criteria, both teachers should play a significant role in establishing guiding questions and points of attention for the visit. As Minter argues in "Peer Observation as Collaborative Classroom Inquiry," many factors—the range of questions, the range of possible purposes for observing, the length and frequency of observations, and so on—affect the kinds of knowledge visits make possible. Consequently, it is important that both teachers shape the form and function of the observation (2002, 86).

In the teaching practicum, we decided that we wanted to use the visits in service of enabling more "reflexive" pedagogy. Rather than the visitor's critiquing the observed according to the terms of his or her own pedagogical values, we saw the visits as an opportunity for both teachers to inquire into their teaching, with the goal of making more deliberate pedagogical choices. Minter makes a distinction between visits that aim to identify shortcomings, which are then ascribed to individual teachers, and those that connect teacher struggles "to a larger, collective challenge that faces all English teachers: How do 'we' enact what we believe about literacy teaching and learning?" (87). It was the latter purpose we wanted our visits to serve.

To this end, we decided our written "observer responses" would position the visiting teacher as a learner, not an evaluator. While this did not foreclose possibilities for critique, it required that we not critique simply because a practice or text was something we disagreed with. For instance, while I might not often lecture in my class, rather than imposing my values or visions onto the classroom I was observing, I was instead to ask: How is lecturing functioning in this class? Why might it be necessary? How are the students responding? In addition to promoting more reflexive "observing," this also helped to reinforce the idea that pedagogies are always highly context-dependent, and that our readings of them need to take into account the local sites in which they take place. Because these contexts are not fully visible to the visitor (or the teacher), we also decided that it would be useful for the observed and the observer to meet afterward, and to discuss how each of them experienced the class. This would give the teacher being observed an opportunity to explain his or her choices, and to fill in some of the contexts.

Our overarching aim was to restructure the visit as a reciprocal dialogue, which both teachers actively took part in designing and from which both would benefit. One problem remained: we would be graded on these interactions by Amy, our practicum leader. We "solved" this by collectively deciding that Amy would not evaluate the teacher being observed, but instead the mode of inquiry engaged by the visitor. Was the observer using the moment as an opportunity to reflect on his or her own teaching? Could he or she demonstrate an ability to think beyond the assumptions and values with which he or she entered the classroom? In this way, Amy's authority was used to encourage learning on the part of the visitor.

Though more complicated because of power differentials, I would contend that establishing shared goals for learning visits is possible even in a more traditional setting, where a WPA visits teachers' classrooms for "official" purposes. Here what becomes especially important is not only examining entrenched notions of the visit, but also *studying the specific institutional and programmatic contexts in which the visits occur*. Often, visits of this kind are perceived as a check on curricular compliance. This will remain the case, I would argue, so long as curricula are conceived as top-down structures, rather than as sites of collaborative design. Though I will discuss this in greater depth in the next section, what's key here is that learning visits be articulated and enacted as opportunities for both the teacher and the WPA to study and negotiate the classroom *and* the curriculum, both understood as in process. For the visitor, the visit becomes a way to learn about the concrete ways the curriculum is being enacted. But the visit also enables an opportunity for dialogue about how each understands the curriculum, how it might best be enacted, which goals are most difficult to realize, and so on.

Of course, this does not change the fact that the WPA is in a position of greater institutional authority than is the part-time instructor or TA. But this authority need not be used oppressively; rather, the WPA can strive to challenge and subvert institutional contexts that promote a top-down structure. For instance, in the program in which I now work, I can call into question the practice whereby only part-time instructors are visited—not only by inviting teachers to my classroom, but by encouraging cross-visiting of one another's classrooms. And while I am required to provide the teacher with a "write-up" of the visit, I can do so in a way that articulates what I have learned from the visit, rather than simply offering a one-way evaluation. Similarly, we can work to challenge the "passive" observer position by coming together to articulate key questions and to establish the foci of the visit, both of which might emerge out of shared interests or problems we encounter in our classrooms. While I do not mean to imply that power differences can be erased, I would argue that the WPA need not be positioned as "owner" of the curriculum.

While every negotiation will be different, the goal is to complicate notions of classroom visits as impositions on private space, and instead to create the conditions whereby they can be mutually beneficial, and, crucially, where both teachers have a stake in their productive enactment.

Composing Curriculum and Community

Participating in any community might feel like compliance unless all members experience their voices as crucial to the discussion; all too often, teachers are asked to comply with curricula, rather than to compose them. As Phelps confirms, teachers at the college level have very limited experience in situations where they "have the solidarity, the power, and the time to make curriculum a medium for their own thinking and learning, as well as that of students" (866). This is largely because in English studies, new teachers are often assigned classrooms within first-year composition programs that have established (and fixed) curricular goals and expectations. They are handed a set syllabus and text that leave little room for their own pedagogical values or visions. The curriculum, ultimately, is owned by the administration, or, often, the university. While subversion of the curriculum may occur on an individual basis, new and innovative ideas are often intentionally kept behind closed doors. We don't, after all, want to invite unnecessary scrutiny.

If graduate students learn compliance with a top-down curriculum in their teaching assistantships, then they learn something altogether different in their seminars. In those curricular spaces, the doctoral student is trained to become a specialist in an area where he or she will, upon achieving professorial status, primarily do research, and with any luck, be able to teach. He or she will act as the department's "owner" of that area of scholarship, as well as of the classroom that serves as its extension. As I've suggested above, this upper-division teaching is likely to occur in a "corporate compromise" curriculum (North 2000), where professors are responsible to their knowledge—or perhaps to the specialized track in which they teach—but not to the curriculum or department as a whole, or to their colleagues in the classrooms surrounding them. This isolation from one another is often conflated with ownership: the professor knows his or her material better than anyone else on the floor, so he or she has the right to determine what and how knowledge is engaged in his or her classroom. To ask the professor to put those individual aims in dialogue with shared goals or values is read, in the research model, as an infringement on his or her freedom.

Indeed, terms like "freedom" and "flexibility" are often used to sell a program to prospective faculty or to part-time teachers. The first-year writing curriculum I inherited as a new WPA touts this flexibility as its greatest strength. In this program, we tell part-time instructors, you can bring your own interests to the classroom (making the course "about" technology or family history or popular culture) and you have a great deal of pedagogical freedom. Indeed, these are important characteristics, and in many ways, contribute to good teaching because they encourage innovation and investment on the part of instructors. However, this freedom easily becomes associated with ownership, so that attempts to discover shared goals and practices are read as threatening and repressive.

I don't blame my colleagues for feeling this way. After all, most of us have been taught in institutions and departments that privilege individual freedom above community commitment. In fact, many us have little or no experience—gaining our teacher training in top-down first-year writing programs and our scholarly training in separate seminars—in imagining what collaborative curriculum building makes possible or even looks like. For this reason, I would like to suggest that we prepare the next generation of professors differently—that they learn, from the start, to think of curriculum not as a fixed structure owned or managed by an administrative "boss," but rather, as Derek Owens describes it, as the "educator's artspace" (2001, 142). Drawing from the architectural visions of Paoli Soleri and Lucien Kroll, Owens promotes a curricular architecture that is an "organic, collaborative, procedural event within a nonhierarchical framework" (146). All "local residents" participate in the design; all are stakeholders in the building process. But as Seitz reminds us, collectivist curricular practice is "easy to call for but terribly difficult to bring about" (2002, 160). In what follows, I will offer specific program practices and considerations that were crucial in enabling both teaching and curriculum development. As always, my aim is to provide not prescriptions, but rather concrete material for reflection.

As a graduate student, I taught in a Writing Sequence made up of five (mostly workshop) courses, taught by six or seven teachers, who ranged from first-time TAs to tenured faculty. The Writing Sequence, like many first-year composition programs, asked teachers to know the curriculum. Unlike many such programs—in which new teachers serve as instruments of the curriculum—our program also asked teachers to contribute to it, even shape it. As a result, it became crucial to establish regular, formal occasions for teachers to come together to reflect on the curriculum. These were designed as two-way interactions, where we considered both how individual courses informed the curriculum and how the curriculum exerted pressure on our individual classrooms. Crucially, though, the curriculum was—had to be—conceived as a work in progress, just as the participants in it—faculty, part-time instructors, TAs, and students—were considered ongoing learners.

In each of our biweekly Writing Sequence teacher meetings, one teacher was asked to facilitate a group discussion concerning a theoretical, pedagogical, practical, or locally specific issue. These questions usually had to do with issues of teaching writing, such as student development, portfolio projects, our conceptions and uses of grading, and so on. In these interactions, we sought to pose questions as, for example, "How should we use grades in the Writing Sequence?" rather than, "How should each of us use grades in our individual classrooms?" While both are important, the distinction is worth examining. The first version of the question implies that a collective decision needed to be made—not that every teacher must use grades in exactly the same way, but that we needed to collectively negotiate the meanings and assumptions informing grading in our curriculum. In the second version of the question, the emphasis is placed on the individual teacher coming to a reflective, deliberate choice about using grades. This is essential, but if we want to provide students with a coherent experience, then it is not sufficient. For that we needed to consider how our individual courses worked within the shared values of the sequence, so that there were shared goals among the courses.

One facilitation, led by Chris, was particularly useful in enabling this study. He asked the following:

> Do the workshops—or all sequence courses, or all 202s—need shared objectives? shared standards? shared pedagogical and as-

sessment practices? If yes, what might these be? If no, how do we ensure some measure of coherence, sequentiality? How much and what kind of coherence do we need? How much teacher autonomy are we willing to give up in order to secure curricular logic and programmatic coherence? (Am I right to assume that there is necessarily a trade-off here?)

What are the programmatic/curricular goals of the sequence course that you are currently teaching? How does it function in the sequence? Thinking of both curriculum and program, what, ideally, would you say students should (a) have done, (b) know, or (c) be able to do when they leave the course that you are teaching?

Our responses indicated a general agreement that students in our classes should develop the following: an ability to read one's own writing critically, and to write about one's writing process; an ability to respond to the writing of other students; a willingness to "try new things" or "experiment" with forms; a more complicated understanding of such cultural terms as "writer," "author," and "literature," as well as an ability to question the function and uses of various forms of writing; and a sense of what it means to participate in a writing community. These were goals we wanted to foster in every Writing Sequence course, and so our next question became how to do so in ways that allowed students to stretch and develop as they moved through the courses.

How, for instance, should 303 and 304, the advanced courses in rhetoric and poetics, build on the introductory course? What should be expected from students in each course? Should it be more work? more "complicated" or sustained writing projects? more of the same? a different kind of writing altogether? But we also wondered about our roles as teachers in the various courses. What should the students expect of us in 202 versus 303? Did we need to be different kinds of readers? Should we be more directive, less directive? Should we be guiding students to produce more polished, publishable texts? Or as they tried new strategies and techniques, should we expect that their writing would become messier, regressing in areas as it developed in others?

Though we did not come up with any final answers in that meeting or in the meetings that followed, we began to realize the challenges the curriculum posed for us, as well as the areas where we would be served by moving closer to shared understandings. For instance, we needed to examine how each of us understood (presumably) shared terms like "development." What is development? How do we know it when we see it? What do we do in our classrooms to enable it? Should we all be engaging in similar practices to enable particular kinds of development?

In the same way, I have sought to create opportunities for reflection on the first-year writing curriculum I now work within. What do we hope students will know or be able to do as a result of enrolling in first-year composition? What experiences do we think all English 150 students should have? What areas of the course can be more flexible? Key here is establishing that the aim of such conversations is not to create a cookie cutter, a mold with which all must comply. Instead it is to establish shared assumptions and values that we all believe in, and which we feel will best serve our students and our program's aims. Of course, it could be argued that this makes more work for part-time teachers or for busy, exploited graduate TAs. I would argue, though—and indeed, I have found—that these opportunities are energizing for participants, because they enable greater investment on the part of the teachers, who see themselves not as cogs in a machine, but as intellectual workers, who are striving on a daily basis to enact a vision they have of an ongoing role in designing.

Of course, while building in moments for teachers to come together to reflect on the development of our individual pedagogies and the curriculum is important, it is not sufficient. We also need to challenge the dynamic whereby some teachers (often those who teach the upper-level courses) are positioned as owners. In the Writing Sequence, we found it useful to change the way course assignments are traditionally granted. That is, professors were not given the "advanced" courses while TAs were assigned the introductory courses. This disrupted the common assumption that, as Seitz puts it, "the most interesting academic work occurs the farther away from introductory courses they move, since the 'higher' they proceed in a curriculum, the greater the amount of knowledge and skill [teachers] can suppose has been previously absorbed by students" (1999, 59). Indeed, we sought to thwart the notion that development is linear and thus that the complexities and difficulties surrounding the acts of read-ing and writing ever really "go away." For this reason, teachers at all levels were required to think about what it meant to engage these activities in each course. The context of each course might be different, but the questions and approaches were not.

Similarly, the sequence aimed to challenge the traditional model that assumes a more experienced teacher is better pre-pared to teach an advanced class, or that a new teacher is quali-fied only to teach an introductory course. In fact, those of us—TAs, part-time instructors, and faculty—who taught the in-troductory course often found it not only to be the most chal-lenging course to teach, but also the most exciting. 202 was the course in which many ideas needed to be challenged, many ques-tions needed to be asked, and much groundwork needed to be established. This is not different from first-year writing, a course that—in addition to being pressured to do an enormous amount of intellectual work—is also commonly met with student resis-tance to the requirement of being there. Faculty members who teach it regularly know what difficult, challenging, and exciting work it is; and this participation is a good hindrance to position-ing oneself as a master teacher.

Collective curriculum building, when it involves participants of various institutional "levels," also requires attention to group dynamics—to the pedagogy of such interactions. How, for in-stance, can we prevent the familiar master-apprentice dynamic from developing in our group? How can we make quality of en-gagement as important as quantity of experience? In the Writing Sequence, we found that productive work was only possible when we shared one essential assumption: each of us was at once a teacher and a learner. This isn't to say that experience did not "count," however; it is rather to indicate that experience is not to be conflated with mastery. Professors are too often positioned institutionally as "finished" teachers, and there are few public or formal contexts in which they are expected, much less encour-aged, to account for pedagogical choices. One of the most diffi-cult aspects of our teaching community, in fact, involved convinc-ing faculty members to reflect on their pedagogies rather than to offer their experiences and choices as prescriptive models.

This was not an easy dynamic to break, and was visible in the ways our facilitations played out. For instance, when professors facilitated, the discussion typically followed a productive and dialogic path, moving between broader, theoretical questions and more specific examples emerging from our classrooms. The theoretical concerns helped us to rethink our local practices, and the questions emerging from our teaching enabled us to exert pressure on our theoretical assumptions. On the other hand, when TAs facilitated, the discussion often shifted to a one-way dynamic in which the new teacher was given "advice" about his or her "problem." Not that these kinds of interactions are never useful, but the facilitations were designed to create an interaction of a different kind.

Disrupting this one-way dynamic was difficult not only because those with more institutional authority continued to exercise it, but also because those of us who were students had trouble redefining ourselves as equal participants in this setting. Freire names this a "fear of freedom" that afflicts the oppressed (1993, 29). In relating his argument to U.S. classrooms, I take this to mean that students—and in this case, new teachers—have learned well to adapt "to the structure of domination in which they are immersed" (29). Consequently, they "have become resigned to it, and are inhibited from waging the struggle for freedom [because] they feel incapable of running the risks it requires" (29). There is safety in the traditional model, which is, more often than not, taken to be natural. Collaborative efforts such as these thus require opportunities to reflect on the meetings themselves, to examine how our aims of collaborative teaching and curriculum building might be hindered by institutional constraints and limited conceptions of our respective roles.

Conversing with Student Contributors

As accepted is the metaphor of professor as classroom owner, there is often great resistance to the notion of students as customers, as it implies that the university is a corporate space. In fact, faculty in English will typically claim an anticorporate stance, insisting that we not turn the integrity of our knowledge over to student interests—customer demands. Ironically, those arguments most strongly in favor of privatization of the classroom are also often most deeply opposed to a consumer model that supposedly "caters" to students. I would argue that both notions are problematic—positioning professors as owners (even when it is couched in terms of academic freedom) and students as customers —because the classroom and curriculum are made into *property*.

Instead, I understand the curriculum and the classrooms within it as shared structures in which students and teachers perform intellectual work together. Neither is the property of one or the other, but instead both are community spaces to which all contribute, and in which all have a stake. This is not to say that faculty can or should turn over their institutional authority, nor is this an argument for students simply "getting" whatever it is they "want." But it *is* to say that professors have the responsibility to enter into dialogue with students about the nature and form of the learning they undertake together. In fact, Gallagher argues that such dialogue is fundamental to "pedagogy-centered" curricula: "Unlike teacher-centered curricula, in which we might lecture to students about empowerment, or student-centered curricula, in which empowerment means 'giving' students freedom to do whatever they like, pedagogy-centered curricula are 'progressive' in the sense that Dewey used the term: they *progress*, they evolve, *through* the dialogue between and among teachers and students" (2002, 164). But what does it mean to invite students into such a dialogue? How can we, as Stenhouse suggests, teach in a style that generates not only acceptance of, but critique of, the curriculum? (70). How can we build moments into the curriculum that enable students opportunity for the kind of reflection necessary to continually further and revise it?

In the Writing Sequence, we learned the importance of structuring into the curriculum opportunities for situated student (and teacher) reflection. Because we wanted to enable students to see the curriculum as working *for* them as much as working *on* them, many of us began our classes by asking students to write both about what they brought to the class as writers, and what they hoped to gain from their participation in it. Going at it a bit differently, Chris developed an assignment that asked students in the introductory course to write a letter, as part of their *final* portfolios, to their next sequence teacher. The letter was intended at once as a way for the student to introduce himself or herself *as a writer* to the new teacher, and also as a space in which the student could reflect, for himself or herself, on his or her development that semester. I see each of these as an important goal. The former is essential in a curriculum that seeks to center itself on the developmental processes of students. Instead of assuming that a teacher can or should predict these needs, however, Chris encouraged the students to articulate those needs for themselves. Similarly, the latter opened a space for the student to evaluate and assess his or her own development and what fostered it, insisting, in a way, that this is not only the job of the teacher, but also of the writer himself or herself. A third function of these letters was to help students articulate how they hoped, in their next course, to build on and develop the ideas and interests raised in Chris's class. In this way, then, Chris's assignment encouraged students to participate in the curriculum, to be contributors, not merely receivers, of the classes they took.

In retrospect, we wish we had made such letters a regular part of every 202 (and subsequent) class, so that students were consistently asked to build conceptual bridges between their courses and to trace the trajectory of their writing development and goals. At the same time, these letters would have allowed teachers to reflect on what students felt worked well in each class, what practices best enabled their development, and how they understood the unfolding of their own developmental paths. And we might have better revised our courses—and the curricular goals—in light of this input.

Though the institutional context is quite different, I have sought to initiate the same kind of dialogue in my first-year writing courses, so as to create a conversation between my individual class and the curriculum. I often begin by asking students to compose a letter to me, describing themselves as writers, naming their semester goals, and articulating what it is they hope to gain from the course. This gives me a sense of their needs and interests and shows me how I can shape the course to help foster these, but it also allows us to examine their expectations and assumptions about how a first-year writing course (and program) should operate. What knowledges, practices, and opportunities do they expect it will, and should, offer? Additionally, we consider the expectations explicitly and implicitly placed on the first-year writing program by the university, since it falls under the "skills" category in our core curriculum. For instance, I tell them, many students and faculty expect that English 150 will once and for all teach students how to learn to write the "academic essay," which they assume can then be transported to any other classroom context. Though I work to disrupt the notion that writing can be finally "learned" in one class, I ask them, at various points in the semester, to share what aspects of the class enable (or make more frustrating) their writing processes in other courses. This helps all of us see what connections are possible among courses.

Near the end of the semester, I ask my students to reflect on how they would describe the development that occurred in their writing over the semester, to consider what practices/activities/ assignments best enabled that development, and to indicate what they would add or change about the course. Because students have been asked throughout the semester not simply to complete the assignments but also to consider what the assignments enable, they are well prepared to speak in thoughtful, insightful ways about why and how aspects of the course worked or didn't. Often, they mention first-year courses that their friends are taking and the assignments engaged there, discussing how such a project might function in our course and the different ways it might enable their writing development. I find, then, that they are already participating in curricular discussions in spaces outside of the course; this is simply a way to invite that discussion inside.

Finally, I make a habit of sharing with my students what the composition committee is discussing about program changes, and of asking for their input, which I then bring back to the committee. Because I have so often heard from students that they wish they knew in advance of a course what the "theme" would be, we made the decision recently to make public our course themes in the catalogue and online. The hope is that this change will allow students greater choices in the selection of courses, and thus greater investment and learning outcomes.

While it is worth considering the critique that including students in curricular conversation might be a form of "pandering" to the customer, it is also important to consider the assumptions that inform this notion—namely, that students are consumers (or children), not intellectual workers. A first step in enabling productive curricular dialogue, then, requires work on the part of faculty members to unpack our conceptions of students' roles. Articulating a metaphor for the writing teacher is a familiar practice in teacher-training settings; here we might articulate and examine the metaphors we would ascribe to the students in our programs. What is at stake in how we understand students? What are the limits and possibilities of our current conceptions? In what ways do our assumptions about students inform how they respond to the curriculum?

Resistance might also stem from the belief that we will be giving students control of our programs. As Gallagher helps us see, though, we need not think about classrooms or curricula as *either* teacher-centered *or* student-centered. Enacting a pedagogy-centered curriculum thus requires both students and teachers to articulate, examine, and assess their needs and interests, and to determine how and where those interests meet. It also creates an opportunity for faculty to articulate to students (and for themselves) how and why the current curriculum takes the shape it does, so that students see the curriculum as a composed, rather than natural, structure. Once this is established, students and teachers can begin to imagine new possibilities within the structure, or to examine potential methods of rebuilding. Of course, this dialogue will look different in each unique institutional context, but faculty and students might be served by first considering several factors: What aspects of the curriculum need to be firmly set in place (and why)? What "practical" constraints exist? What aspects might be more flexible? What vehicles exist for students and faculty to propose course ideas? to reflect on current structures?

These practices might likely be read as threatening, since they open the curriculum up for critique. Again, they make public what we assume is (or hope will be) private. But in doing so, we also open the door to new ideas and to curriculum development that will enable greater investment on the parts of both students and faculty. I am suggesting, then, that we work now to establish more formalized opportunities for faculty-student dialogue, and that we teach the next generation of professors, from the start, to see student input as a vital component of pedagogical, classroom, and curricular development.

The Local and the Disciplinary

The practices I offer in the chapter—learning visits, collective curriculum and community building, and student-teacher dialogue—are designed not only to challenge the privatization of classrooms and curricula, but to promote critical dialogue that serves to unearth "common commitments and understandings" (Phelps 1991, 867). Once we discover what is shared across classrooms—a common project in which all are invested—then everyone gains a stake in ongoing teacher and curriculum development. Rather than serving as a "check" on how well teachers are complying with top-down structures, community activities instead serve to foster a mutual commitment, a collaborative enterprise.

Of course, community activities do not function apart from institutional dynamics and expectations, and these dynamics need to be made visible as communities are built and enacted. This has become particularly clear in my department, now that the dean has issued a mandate that each department in our college create a form of teaching assessment to supplement the student evaluations. Our department is now at work to implement visits that we hope will function in formative—not just summative—ways. In doing so, we have returned to the guidelines created for part-time visits, which are designed primarily to support the developmental needs and interests of the teacher being visited. We want the visits to be meaningful to those involved in them, not a mere vehicle for meeting an administrative mandate. But as several of my colleagues have asked, "How does the visitor write a letter that is at once developmental and that helps demonstrate the success of the teacher?" Many expressed a felt tension between providing a letter that is formative and one that reports to the dean that this teacher is successful (and deserves a raise). Of course, the stakes are higher for those of us who aren't yet tenured. Is it possible to enact the visit and subsequent report in a manner that is developmental and not merely evaluative? One of my colleagues offered a wise insight: We need to convince the dean that engaging in developmental work signals teaching success. Rather than presenting ourselves as "finished" teachers, we need to trust that we can show the dean (and tenure committees) that we are all teachers in process, committed to reflection and revision.

Whether we will convince the dean of this remains to be seen, but it is one example of the role that those of us in composition can play in convincing our colleagues and administrators of the importance of collaborative practitioner inquiry. By changing our minds and our behaviors, we change the way disciplinarity is enacted. By teaching the next generation and our colleagues different disciplinary practices, we work toward a new disciplinary enterprise. In the next chapter, I will propose and offer examples of disciplinarity that center on learning encounters, and that position the professor as an ongoing learner.

The Teacher as Learner

A s I have argued throughout this book, professorial identity is inextricably linked to disciplinary identity. As long as the discipline functions as a gated community that opens its doors only to contributing scholars, teacher development will remain isolated from professorial preparation. Changing the value placed on teaching—and thus the emphasis placed on teacher preparation—requires a simultaneous shift in our conceptions and enactments of disciplinarity.

During the last two decades, scholars in composition and rhetoric have devoted much attention to the field's relationship to disciplinarity. Some argue that our pedagogy-centered values establish us as an alternative or postdisciplinary enterprise (Harkin 1991; Slevin 1996; Farris and Anson 1998) and others contend that we have bought into the lure of disciplinarity at the price of part-time teacher exploitation (Vandenberg 1998; Connors 1999; Ferry 1998; Trimbur 1996). While both sides make compelling cases, one thing is certain: composition has an ambivalent and fraught relationship to disciplinarity. This, I would contend, is not a negative position—in fact, the tension we experience between wanting, as Gallagher puts it, the "trappings" of disciplinarity (the journals, the graduate and undergraduate programs, the tenure-track lines, the feeling of inclusion) and resisting the "trap" (the "containment and normalization" of our intellectual work and the devaluing of teaching) might help us to maintain a critical and self-reflexive stance toward normative disciplinarity as we work toward an alternative vision (2002, 109).

In this chapter, I will weigh in on this particular debate by arguing that we can take advantage of those characteristics that make composition distinct in order to promote and extend a model of disciplinarity—and of professing—that values activities of teaching and learning. I contend that we can do so in two ways: through our work with graduate students on *initial* teacher development and through our work with colleagues across the subfields of English studies (including advanced TAs) on *ongoing* teacher development. If we can help the next group of professors to reimagine the role of pedagogy as crucial to their professorial lives, the hope is that they will enact disciplinarity differently, exerting pressure on its current shape. And if we can invite our colleagues to engage in ongoing teacher-development opportunities, we can form collectives around pedagogy that help to alter our professorial work and foster disciplinary revision. After all, promoting pedagogy as intellectual work cannot, indeed should not, rest only on the shoulders of those of us in composition.

Composition's Disciplinary (Re)Vision

We might begin this disciplinary revisioning by making visible to new teachers and colleagues how composition goes about its academic business differently. Slevin offers perhaps the most generous version of this work, contending that composition abides by the most traditional, or original, meaning of discipline, which derives from the Latin word *discipulus,* or "learner" (1996, 156). In its original form, the discipline actually privileged the act of teaching and learning over a body of scholarship:

> [The discipline] involved "instruction imparted to disciples or scholars; teaching; learning; education, schooling": a meaning the Oxford English Dictionary now declares "obsolete." In contrast to the knowledge imparted (called "doctrine," which comes from *docere,* which also gives us, among other words, "doctor"), discipline entailed the activities of imparting and learning. [. . .] At the heart of the real work in a discipline was not the scholar (or doctor, concerned with doctrine) but the learner and the teacher who helped that learning. (156)

While there is much evidence to suggest that composition has not achieved this learning-centered model of disciplinarity (the most incriminating being the great economic divide between tenure-track composition "professionals" and part-time or "adjunct" teachers), we can also readily find confirmation that this vision is vital and viable in composition.

For instance, the feature that most distinguishes composition from its disciplinary siblings is its primary focus on pedagogy, and, more specifically, its conception of pedagogy as a mode of knowledge production, not merely a vehicle for knowledge transmission. As I've suggested in earlier chapters, other areas of English studies are beginning to embrace this view, but it is, and always has been, a cornerstone of composition. Our focus on pedagogy—whereby our activities of teaching and learning inform and shape our scholarship—helps protect our field from functioning as a normative discipline, with a static body of guarded knowledge. This is not to say that our discipline does not offer important and useful scholarship that abides by current disciplinary rules and regulations, or that all scholarship must emerge from the site of the classroom. Rather, it is to suggest that scholarship should not function as a gated and static body of knowledge, but should remain open to the pressures placed on it by teacher-learner collaborations.

One result of this pedagogical "pressure" is a growing body of work representing new voices, approaches and forms, which have potential to challenge the divisive line between teaching and research. Teacher narratives, collages, case studies of student writing, and literacy ethnographies grow increasingly visible in our field (a list that includes, but is certainly not limited to, Rose 1989; Heath 1983; Knoblauch and Brannon 1993; Welch 1993; Boquet 2002; Lee 2000; Cushman 1998; Gallagher 2002; Sternglass 1997; Qualley 1997; Malinowitz 1995; Ritchie and Wilson 2000; Kameen 2000). The recent collection *Alt Dis: Alternative Discourses and the Academy* (Schroeder, Fox, and Bizzell 2002) offers an array of texts that not only represent new forms of intellectual work but also call attention to the limits of normative academic discourse. Collectively, these texts challenge many familiar dichotomies: academic/nonacademic; professional/personal; teaching/research. Of course, it should not go without saying here that it is often only tenure-track faculty who have the time and resources to contribute to this published dialogue.

While we (and those who guard the disciplinary gates) still have a way to go in valuing "alternative discourse"—including scholarship that makes pedagogy its subject or that is based on knowledge produced in the classroom—we can at least claim that our field's scholarship is always under revision, in both form and function (North 1996). It is important that this revision is sparked by interaction not only among scholars, but also teachers and learners.

We can also look to graduate curricula in composition and rhetoric to see evidence that even within traditional programs and institutions, we teach our discipline differently. In their seminars, composition graduate students are typically given a chance to integrate the scholarly and the pedagogical, to bring their teaching to bear on their coursework and vice versa. Composition students' work as teachers is not designated as a mere source of funding their "real" academic work, but as a site of intellectual inquiry that can and should function in dialogue with their coursework.

Now I would like to see us confront the teaching/research binary in teacher-development sites. As I have suggested throughout this book, we need to rethink our pedagogies in initial development sites—the one place where graduate students from all subdivisions of English studies come together. But we need also to create opportunities for the ongoing development of experienced teachers—that is, to create sites in which teachers (professors, part-time instructors, TAs) can came together to work in and on pedagogy.

To be sure, many WPAs already enact innovative teacher-development programs that seek to challenge the disciplinary status quo. Conversations with colleagues across the country assure me this is the case, and in what follows, I will represent some of this rich and exciting work. However, this work is not often made public, since issues of teacher development still remain marginalized, even during English studies' "pedagogical turn" (Downing 1994). And those teacher-training pieces that *are* made public tend to reinforce the conception of pedagogy either as a set of skills to be acquired—a move that relegates teaching to a space outside of the discipline—or as a body of knowledge to be mastered—making pedagogy yet another body of knowledge in the discipline.

Contributing to both the traditional shape and the relative lack of postsecondary teacher-development scholarship are the institutional contexts of this work. That is, as much as teacher-scholars in composition have worked to challenge the teaching/research binary, the conditions for teacher training often set us up to perpetuate this divide; they still require us to *train* teachers, rather than to enable their lifelong pedagogical *development*. Those who prepare future faculty members and teaching assistants still do so under great time (and budget) constraints and on the margins of graduate (and first-year writing) curricula. While many WPAs want to foster the development of part-time instructors—and many part-time instructors are interested in such opportunities—the demand for excellent undergraduate teaching in our required courses is rarely matched with funding for teacher-development programs, or with compensation for overworked and underpaid part-timers. Consequently, even if the good intention is there, as I believe it typically is, we are not always able to create opportunities for new teachers (let alone experienced teachers) to engage pedagogy as an ongoing, disciplinary enterprise.

In what follows I argue for the conceptual and pedagogical shift from teacher training to teacher development. I then articulate several key characteristics of learning encounters designed to foster teacher development, which are followed by examples of this work. Finally, I examine the conceptual, pedagogical, and material work required to make teaching and learning central disciplinary activities.

Developing (in) the Learning-Centered Discipline

If we are to enact a learning-centered discipline that "exists in acts of instruction and discussion," Slevin contends, those who participate in the discipline must "know how to teach" (1996, 159). His vision is worth quoting at length:

> At the heart of the educational practice I propose is a reconcept-ualizing of disciplinarity so that its intellectual work is located in encounters with students and in the projects that arise from these encounters. What we need is a sense of disciplinary work that

> supports and even makes possible these developments, a sense of "discipline" that allows literacy workers (teachers and students) in various institutional sites (academic and nonacademic) to feel the importance of what they do and to recognize their connections with one another. (160)

We need, in other words, professors who not only "know how to teach," but also are able to invite students into disciplinary encounters, to work collaboratively with students on pedagogy, and to study, reflect on, and alter their pedagogical approaches. Clearly, this model of disciplinarity requires a new approach to preparing future English professors. But it also requires that professors and TAs participate in ongoing learning opportunities, so as to continue to "recognize [and discover] their connections" with one another as teachers.

Those of us in composition might initiate these efforts by insisting, in the sites in which we now work, on a conceptual and pedagogical shift from teacher *training* to teacher *development*. As I've discussed in previous chapters, current methods of teacher training tend to promote either an inner, intellectual growth (via acquisition of the correct knowledge) or an outer, social acculturation (via acquisition of the skills required to adapt to a curriculum) (Haswell 1991). Training is necessarily a one-way interaction wherein only the (new) teacher is required to change. This model coheres with normative disciplinarity, positioning pedagogy as either a subject matter to consume or a skill to master and thus preserving the hierarchy between professor (who has the knowledge or skills) and student (who needs the knowledge or skills). This is not to say, however, that practices typically associated with "training"—orientations, teaching practica, etc.—are inherently problematic. In orientations or initial training sessions, new teachers are often given what they most claim to need to get started as teachers: *effective* practices (with well-developed theories informing them) and *affective* confidence. The problem is that these practices are often considered an end, rather than a beginning.

I would contend, then, that we might present our initial interactions with new teachers as the beginning of a lifetime process of teacher development, which differs greatly from the

one-way and masterable process of training. Teacher *development* requires a dialogue among new teacher, experienced teacher,
and the field, with all three open to revision. Richard Haswell,
describing writing development, explains this concept well:

> [Development] is not just an inner, maturational growth nor just
> an outer, social acculturation, nor even an interaction between
> the two, but an educational life-process or lifework composed of
> three main forces or vectors, all on the move. Where the develop-
> ment of student, field of writing, and teacher meet and are fur-
> thered by the meeting, there genuine educational development
> takes place. (1991 5)

Educational sites that promote development, then, need to prepare teachers to be disciplinary contributors and learners and to
create mutually beneficial encounters with others, which might
even transform the field. This requires that we invite new teachers to participate in ongoing inquiry, to encounter an ever-present
series of changes in themselves, their students, the classroom, the
field. But it also requires those of us who profess (whether pedagogy or American literature) to occupy the position of teacher as
learner, to remain open to the possibility of change during each
learning encounter. Of course, this also means we need opportunities for teacher learning that reach far beyond the initial orientation, practicum, and seminar—and that are designed for, and
led by, a greater range of teacher-scholars in English studies.

Teaching as Learning

In previous chapters, I have challenged models of teacher preparation centered upon acquisition of scholarship, orientation to
predetermined curricular or programmatic goals and practices,
and/or ownership of one's classroom. Instead, I have argued for
encounters with pedagogical scholarship that portray the teacher
as ongoing learner, opportunities to reflect on the relationship
between the pedagogies from which we've learned and the
pedagogies we seek to enact, and teacher learning that is equally
dependent upon community and curriculum. In this chapter, I
continue to promote these (re)visions by featuring several key

characteristics of teacher learning that are essential for moving beyond normative modes of disciplinarity and for promoting teacher development. Learning encounters designed to foster teacher development do the following:

◆ Position new (and part-time) teachers as knowers: As I have argued throughout the book, new teachers do not enter training sites as blank slates, but with their own (often implicit or unexpressed) pedagogies. It is the role of the teacher-development site to help new teachers make visible these pedagogies and revise them as they see fit, but the interaction need not be one-way. We need, that is, to create encounters that foster the mutual development of teachers across traditional boundaries of "status" (i.e., full- versus part-time, administrator versus teacher) and position each group as (at once) knower and learner.

◆ Create opportunities to make teaching public for reflection and revision: A teacher-learner approaches his or her classroom as always under construction. Often the greatest opportunities for revision are discovered through supportive and critical dialogue with other teachers. By creating opportunities for teachers to share their work with colleagues, we not only teach the important practice of collaborative reflection and revision but also transform the notion that teaching is a private activity.

◆ Enable teachers to participate in conversations across traditional institutional and disciplinary boundaries: Learning-centered disciplinarity requires us to challenge the idea that only professors of English can prepare the discipline's future teachers. It is important, then, to invite teachers to participate in dialogue with those often excluded from teacher-training or disciplinary sites (e.g., tutors in the writing center, high school teachers, literacy educators in the community, teachers of writing in other disciplines). By initiating conversations with literacy sponsors from a variety of sites, we broaden our access to new ways of teaching and learning.

Teaching Learning Encounters

While I am not sure that I can fully buy into Slevin's notion that composition already functions as a learning-centered discipline, I do know that it is not difficult to locate examples of learning-centered encounters within our field. It is this work, which both fosters teacher development and challenges traditional notions of disciplinarity, that gives me hope that, even if yet unreached, an alternative disciplinarity is attainable.

In what follows, I offer representations of ongoing teacher-development practices from institutions ranging from a two-year college in New York City to a land-grant research university in Nebraska. Each example was chosen because it extends beyond teacher training to teacher development at the same time that it challenges entrenched notions of the discipline. In inviting colleagues to describe these interactions, my hope is not only to provide rich examples for readers to engage, but also to enact the kind of dialogue for which I argue; this chapter, itself, might serve as an example of such an "encounter" among teachers. While each example is designed to highlight one of the characteristics featured in the above section, they are in no way mutually exclusive; often a single practice enables multiple opportunities.

Positioning New Teachers as Knowers

If traditional disciplinary dynamics position the professor as knower and the student as empty vessel, then traditional teacher-training dynamics position the experienced teacher (or professor or writing program administrator) as master and the new (or part-time) teacher as apprentice. The professor or administrator gives the new teacher the knowledge or skills necessary to operate within a (fixed) curriculum; the dynamic is necessarily one-way. In a learning-centered discipline, teachers are positioned, to borrow Brian Lord's term, as "critical colleagues," who serve "as commentators and critics of their own or other teachers' practices" (1994, 185). Crucially, though, for this relationship to function, there must be a sense of reciprocity and trust, since the expectation is that teachers will come together to learn from one another, to share successes, problems, and practices, but also to engage in "productive disequilibrium through self-reflection, collegial dialogue, and ongoing critique" (192). One step toward enacting a reciprocal relationship involves altering the fixed positions of knower and learner, instead creating opportunities for those typically positioned as "clients" to function as authorities.

The example that follows describes one such effort in promoting critical colleagueship:

AMY LEE, GENERAL COLLEGE, UNIVERSITY OF MINNESOTA

This spring, we inaugurated a new model of teacher development in our writing program. Previously, we had gathered each fall for a few intense days. Those sessions were "led" (and thus conceptualized and designed) by one of the program's directors. We tried to make them as interactive as we could and to include topics that would speak to our teachers' interests and needs. And yet we kept running into a familiar roadblock: How could we generate more organic session ideas, rather than imposing them in a top-down fashion? I couldn't shake the sense that we were doing "programming," rather than supporting development.

Last year, Karen Connolly-Lane, the assistant director, suggested that we should invite every teacher, in groups of two to four, to design sessions for our development workshops. This way, teachers would have the experience of collaborating in the small groups as they prepared, as well as in the large group when they facilitated. This model thus provided multiple occasions for sharing the ideas, philosophies, and challenges of our teaching. We decided to emphasize "facilitation," stressing that we did not expect (or encourage) people to present papers, asking teachers to think about the pedagogy of their sessions and not just the topics. How would they be inviting us into a discussion or activity? How was the session modeling a way of teaching and not just a new idea or practice or problem? Also worth noting is that we decided to meet in May, just after school ended, rather than in August a few days before school began. This would provide time for reflecting on and incorporating the ideas.

Once Karen and I began fleshing out this idea of a conference, it seemed quite obvious and useful—a familiar forum to those of us in academe, but used here to present thinking about our teaching instead of our scholarship. There was, as might be expected, initial resistance on the part of our teaching staff. Rather than wish the resistance away, we met it head-on. I sent out an e-mail in which I noted that people seemed skeptical and talked about why. I acknowledged that this would be more work for everyone, but it was intended to be beneficial, meaningful work. Ideally, the conference would enable people to talk together and thus help us form a stronger sense of teaching community. It would also make more visible the good work occurring in our individual classes as well as stimulate our own teaching. I thanked people for doing the work in advance and asked them to be willing to give this a genuine try.

The conference itself was even more successful than we had hoped. Most teachers participated in multiple facilitations and we engaged a broad range of topics: ethics; behavioral issues; models for peer review; course design; teacher's attitudes and assumptions; working with nonnative speakers; classroom dynamics; working with texts that challenge students in various ways. The topics were familiar, but because they came from everyone, and because the manner of facilitation varied so greatly, the topics came across differently, even for someone like me who has been attending orientations and development workshops for twelve years.

The evaluations of the conference-model were unequivocally positive. Our teaching staff (faculty, adjunct, and graduate student alike) talked not only about the ideas, tools, and possibilities they took from the sessions, but also about how the conference format itself made them feel a part of something. They said they felt valued, respected and more fully enfranchised by this model.

While leading a workshop or conference session may feel overwhelming to someone who is brand-new to teaching, participating in this encounter would certainly offer benefits. Participation would likely help answer new teachers' oft-expressed need for ideas, practices, and strategies that "work," and it would give them a sense of how the program is enacted by teachers in individual classrooms. It is important, though, that in a model like the pedagogy conference, these ideas would be offered as sites of discussion and inquiry for both new and experienced teachers to reflect upon, not as top-down prescriptions. Moreover, participating in the conference might give new teachers (who here are from multiple disciplines, not just composition or even English) a concrete example of what it means to engage pedagogy as intellectual inquiry, work that can be done by all—new and experienced—teachers.

This conference also serves as an opportunity for ongoing development, both for experienced teachers and for program directors. Once teachers move past "initiation" stages, there are rarely formal opportunities for ongoing learning and for discussion of how a program is enacted by individual teachers. This conference allows teachers to articulate different approaches to a shared course, but it also gives administrators insight into how individual teachers animate the program's goals and objectives. Both opportunities foster potential for growth and change, not only in individual pedagogies, but also in the curriculum as a whole.

Creating Opportunities to Make Teaching Public for Reflection and Revision

After TAs complete their apprenticeships in training or orientation sites, their work tends to be largely invisible. Since first-year writing exists on the margins of the English curriculum, and since the assistantship itself is seen to serve only as a source of funding for one's "real" graduate (course) work, there is rarely reason for TAs to make public their classroom work. While anyone who has been a TA knows that rich and rousing teacher dialogue occurs regularly in their crowded office spaces, it is nonetheless "informal" and separate from their credit-bearing doctoral work.

In the next example, I draw from the work of Amy Goodburn, who seeks to counter this privatization of first-year writing teaching. After participating in (and eventually leading) a faculty peer review of teaching project, which allows faculty members to create course portfolios and exchange ideas and suggestions with one another, Amy extended this project to TAs of first-year writing. What follows is her letter of invitation to the program:

AMY GOODBURN, UNIVERSITY OF NEBRASKA, LINCOLN

Dear [Teaching Assistant]:

I write to invite you to participate in the First-Year Writing Course Portfolio Project for the 2002–03 academic year. The Course Portfolio Project is an initiative designed to support teachers of first-year writing courses in documenting and reflecting upon their goals for teaching and their students' performance/ learning. You have been asked to participate in this select group because of your prior success in teaching first-year writing courses and your overall contributions to the English Department teaching community.

This project is based on the work of UNL's Peer Review of Teaching Project, which has supported teachers for the past ten years in documenting and reflecting upon their teaching. The project is designed to support you (within a community of other teachers) to develop a *course portfolio* that focuses on your teaching and your students' learning within an English 150 or 151 course. The project would also promote conversation with other teachers about common teaching and curricular issues in 150/151.

What would my participation in this project entail?

◆ During the fall semester, you would write two memos (of about three to four pages each) in which you discuss the goals/aims of your course and the pedagogical practices/teaching techniques you use to achieve these goals. You would also collect samples of all student work from six or seven randomly selected students in your course (with their permission).

◆ During the spring semester, you would write one memo (of about five to six pages) in which you analyze the student work you collected during the fall, focusing on how well your students' work meets the learning objectives you described in the first two memos. Once the third memo is complete, you would write an integrative reflective analysis regarding your overall experience as a means of creating a course portfolio for your teaching of the 150 or 151 course.

◆ During both fall and spring semesters, you would meet twice with other participants to share and respond to one another's memos and to continue conversation about issues related to teaching and improving student learning.

The prompts you would use to write your memos are represented at the UNL Peer Review Web site (unl.edu.peerrev). These prompts will be slightly scaled down to help us focus more specifically on the goals/pedagogical practices commonly used in 150 and 151. On this Web site you can also see sample course portfolios produced by other UNL teachers. While these portfolios have been converted to electronic formats, the portfolios that you produce will remain text-based.

How will I benefit from this project?

During the project, you will have an opportunity to reflect upon your teaching in a way that will lead to better understanding of student learning and performance. Participants in the Peer Review Project often comment that the experience helps them to modify and revise their teaching both during the semester that they are teaching the course as well as in subsequent course offerings. By the end of this project, you will have created a course portfolio that you can use to represent your teaching to other audiences (e.g., for the job market or merit reviews). Some teachers have disseminated their work via university presentations, conference papers, and journal articles. In addition, you will receive an honorarium of $400 upon completion of your course portfolio.

How will my course portfolio be used by the department?

1. The composition program may use these portfolios in the presemester workshop for new teaching assistants as a means of showcasing student work typically produced in first-year writing courses. It may also draw upon this work in developing materials for 150/151 teachers.

2. The English Department Assessment Committee may use these portfolios as a means of documenting student performance/learning in first-year writing courses.

3. The English Department Program Review Committee might refer to these portfolios to illustrate the type(s) of writing commonly undertaken within first-year writing courses and to provide baselines of student performance within these courses.

Ultimately, you will be the author of your course portfolio and will decide how you would like your work disseminated to other audiences. For any of these purposes, you would have the choice of remaining anonymous.

I hope you seriously consider this invitation to participate. Beyond the excellent teachers, the department would greatly benefit from your expertise.

Sincerely,

Amy Goodburn, Composition Coordinator

This project enables teachers (new and experienced) in multiple ways: it teaches them to document their work (which, as Amy notes, is useful for job applications or merit reviews); it creates a formal opportunity for reflection; it invites teachers to exchange ideas; and it allows teaching assistants, who are often invisible laborers, to make their important work visible.

At the same time, this practice challenges normative conceptions of disciplinarity. In addition to making explicit graduate students' teaching as intellectual work, this project is founded on the idea that teachers' articulations of their pedagogical visions and practices can and should help administrators better understand and facilitate the first-year writing curriculum. In this way, the project not only facilitates individual teacher development, but fosters curriculum (and administrative) development, as well.

This project could certainly make up part of initial teacher development, if TAs were given adequate time and compensation. After all, it is never too early to begin to reflect on and document one's teaching. But it also serves as an important opportunity for ongoing professorial development, as well. In fact, Amy participated, along with another colleague in composition and two in literature, in a similar portfolio project designed to foster not only individual reflection on teaching, but also a discussion of pedagogical visions, values, and outcomes with other teachers in her department.

Whether for initial or ongoing development, the opportunity to create and share course portfolios enables important moments of dialogue and collaboration among teachers who may represent different areas of the field. Since teaching is our primary shared activity in English studies, these moments of collaboration that allow us to see into one another's classrooms not only facilitate reflection, but can also fuel discussion about how our pedagogies speak to one another.

Enabling Cross-Boundary Dialogue

As I suggest above, one crucial component of fostering a learning-centered discipline is inviting in, as knowers, those who are not traditionally included in disciplinary conversations. It is also important to reach across institutional boundaries to learn with and from those who work in sites traditionally granted second-class or "outsider" status (e.g., high school teachers, writing center tutors, community literacy sponsors). As Gallagher contends, outreach projects, while an important part of composition's history, are rarely a part of our contemporary work. When university and school instructors do interact, it is often in a service relationship, whereby the university professor acts as expert and school teacher as passive recipient (2002, 187).[1] The next example demonstrates the fruitfulness of cross-institutional learning between college and high school teachers. In the project described below, this dynamic is challenged in a way that serves the development of all participants involved.

City University of New York, Learning Both Ways

Learning Both Ways is a four-year-old professional development project at the City University of New York (CUNY) designed to enable collaboration between college and high school teachers. The program is not, as George Otte writes, intended to provide initial "training"; rather, it usually includes experienced teachers who are often in charge of professional and curricular development in their respective institutions (2002, 114). In this way, it promotes ongoing development for experienced teachers and administrators who can then bring their new insights to bear on their work with teachers at their home institutions. This is not to say, however, that new(er) teachers (who most often teach the first-year course) could not benefit from a similar experience, if given adequate time and compensation.

LBW creates opportunities for cross-institutional learning, approaches professional development as inquiry (not training), encourages sharing teacher and student work, and positions teachers as readers and writers themselves. Their work now includes scholarly research projects, publications, a Web site, and a conference. While a more extensive description of this project can be found at http://lbw.cuny.edu/ or in the site's *LBW Book: High School and College Teachers Talk about Language and Learning,* I will focus here on one component of their project: intervisitations, classroom visits between high school and college teachers, which Otte describes as the "profoundest experience for most people involved in the LBW project" (116). The LBW Web site gives us some insight into why this experience is imperative for teachers:

> [Intervisitations are] one of the most important activities in enabling teachers to "look both ways," since they experience one another's teaching contexts in both their institutional and classroom dimensions. No one who makes a visit to the "other" institution leaves unchanged.
>
> In the first year, we found high school teachers were at times appalled to see the conditions that accompanied teaching at some

CUNY campuses; others were struck by the freedom that accompanied college teaching. College teachers, likewise, had their eyes opened. Most came to LBW with little knowledge of NYC high schools. Most shared the perceptions commonly perpetuated in the media: schools are rough and noisy; teachers spend most of their time disciplining students; no one does much of substance.

> After their visits to the high schools, and after spending time in their colleague's classrooms, no college instructor would claim that high school teachers do not teach with passion and conviction. In fact, each group of teachers saw how much it had to learn from the other; all felt grateful to have demolished long-standing stereotypes and to leave LBW seminars with increased respect for one another's jobs as well as a deeper recognition of the teaching tasks and goals they share. (http://lbw.cuny.edu/how/visiting/index.html)

After completing the intervisitations, high school and college teachers are invited to reflect on their experiences; some of these reflections are posted on the LBW Web site at http://lbw.cuny.edu/how/visiting. In these reflections, we can see how these encounters changed both groups of teachers. As Gail Kleiner writes in "Getting to Know Each Other's Institutions," the intervisitations were the first opportunity college and high school teachers had to "counter negative views of each other, to challenge misconceptions" (1999, 13). They developed a richer understanding of the complex conditions that enable and constrain both institutional sites, and consequently, a greater empathy and respect for one another.

College teachers were made aware, for instance, of the lack of autonomy high school teachers experience as a result of the state standards and regents' exams. Kleiner names it an "extreme top-down approach to controlling teachers and curriculum in the hopes of attaining high standards for all students" (16). On the other hand, high school teachers came to see that CUNY instructors experience the opposite problem: a lack of dialogue among faculty, an autonomy so extreme as to produce a feeling of working in isolation, and little accountability (16). Of course, this not only enabled teachers to better understand the conditions of one another's work, but also the contexts shaping their students' learning.

Consequently, they were able to focus more closely on students' experiences as they move from high school to college, and to begin discussion about how to better facilitate this transition. There is, in other words, always a common goal at play: to foster students' learning. In these intervisitations teachers are given the opportunity to develop and grow so as to enable students' development. And just as this project fosters teacher learning, it also fosters disciplinary change. As Otte writes, "Teaching is a paradoxical endeavor in that it is always a public performance [. . .] that is also a closeted activity. Teachers know remarkably little about how other teachers teach; this is true of their own colleagues, still more true of the teachers who taught the students before or will teach them after" (116). This project challenges that paradox in order to facilitate dialogue and mutual development.

While the participation of first-year writing faculty is logical here, it need not be limited to those in composition. After all, the more we understand how students have learned, the better we are able to meet their needs and facilitate their development in all of the courses we teach.

Gatekeepers and Institutional Gates

I offer these examples not only to argue for learning encounters that promote ongoing teacher development and challenge the disciplinary status quo, but also to show that such practices are already being enacted. While I hope they will spark ideas for readers, they are not intended as models—largely because they are not simply transportable. Each of the contributors had to negotiate specific institutional contexts and constraints to make these encounters possible. In nearly all of the above cases, someone (usually the WPA) had to argue the case for teaching to administrators so as to receive funding or curricular space. To engage some of these projects without funding would have done as much to reinforce the status quo as to challenge it.

If teaching and teacher development are to be valued as much as scholarly development, then we need to reward it, to make it "count," whether by offering credit or monetary compensation.

For those of us who direct writing programs or vote on curricular decisions, this means advocating not only for these teacher-development opportunities, but also for their sanctioning by the department or college. This is no easy task, especially as budgets are tight and overworked WPAs (many of whom are, like me, untenured) not only have limited time and energy to fight these battles, but may also operate under the understandable fear that challenging the status quo may threaten their job security.

Even so, I believe we need not perceive our dilemma as either/or: either accommodate the "system" or reject it and risk one's program or even job. Instead, we can use the (relative) institutional power and our disciplinary (and rhetorical) training to work at once within and against institutional structures. In her book *The Struggle and the Tools,* Ellen Cushman examines the ways some community gatekeepers use their authority to foster democratic possibility even as they work within a system that too often perpetuates inequity. As I've demonstrated throughout this book, the professor has long occupied the role of disciplinary gatekeeper, guarding the boundaries of the field and limiting the entry of certain knowledges and subjects. With Cushman I agree that we can use this position and power to different ends. We can, she argues, "(a) consciously build upon the institutional language tools we have; (b) deploy them carefully, paying special attention to the politics of our interactions and maintaining respect for the history and culture of our students [. . .] and colleagues [or TAs, part-time teachers, etc.]; and (c) assess and revamp our language tools especially when our exchanges don't go as planned" (1998, 237). In other words, we can make use of institutionally sanctioned tools to challenge that which denies teaching its proper disciplinary place.

While there are unfortunately no fail-proof or standardized strategies to advocate for material change in our institutions, a crucial first step involves what Gallagher calls "institutional literacy," which he defines this way: "To be institutionally literate is to be able to read institutional discourses (and their resultant arrangements and structures) so as to speak and write back to them, thereby participating in their revision. [. . .] Institutional literacy is not metaphorical; institutions are in fact sets of discourses that must be read and written by their participants" (2002,

79, 80). We might compare developing institutional literacy with developing awareness of the rhetorical contexts we write within: What are the limits and possibilities of this discourse? Who are the central speakers? What is the tone of the dialogue? How has it been altered and by whom?

For those of us who come fresh out of graduate schools into administrative positions, institutional literacy might be facilitated by making contacts within and beyond the department to learn about institutional nuances, about how changes have been made in the past, what rhetorical moves are most effective, what will and won't be heard. It might also mean establishing community with WPAs beyond one's institution, who can narrate their own paths of negotiation, offering ideas and support. For me, this has been crucial, as my collaboration with writing directors from a local state university and a community college has helped me, among other things, to gather factual information about the discrepancy between our salaries for part-time instructors and those at other institutions, and then to make a case to the dean for raises. While the concrete, numerical facts were certainly essential to this argument, I believe that speaking as part of a WPA "collective" also served my case.

We can also challenge disciplinary gates by making visible to the next generation of professors the processes and practices we undertake in working within and against disciplinary structures. Like the traditional discipline, institutions are composed of a set of discourses and texts in which we can intervene. Just as we help students negotiate ways of entering and contributing to scholarly conversations, we can also help them consider how to enter and contribute to institutional contexts. For instance, the director of the writing curriculum I taught within as a graduate student made a regular practice of sharing with students and teachers alike the proposals and plans involved in designing the curriculum. This not only helped us to understand the pedagogical underpinnings of the program, but also allowed us to consider the compromises he had to make so that the curriculum would be approved (e.g., including a large, lecture-style capstone course to "pay" for the fifteen-person workshops at the lower level). To achieve his vision, which in many ways worked against the pedagogical norms of a large research institution, he had to work both within and against institutional structures; by making this process of negotiation public, he helped us see the institution, however stubborn, as nonetheless alterable.

Embracing the Mess of Learning

If learning-centered encounters are to function productively, we need to challenge not only material realities, but also the conceptions we may hold about what constitutes a valuable learning experience. Certainly the process, and even the results, of learning encounters are not likely to be as neat and tidy as those of traditional teacher-training approaches. Orientation and training sessions, after all, are designed to offer skills and practices that "orient" the new teacher, make him or her comfortable in a new setting. This is certainly important for a new teacher who is nervous and who needs assistance in beginning the work of teaching. But training implies that mastery is the desired end—that completion and comfort in one's expertise is the final goal. Development, on the other hand, requires us to embrace the mess, since growth requires some discomfort.

We know that a pedagogy that relies on all of its participants and makes students' ideas central is riskier and more complicated than a course in which students simply receive and are tested upon knowledge transmitted by the professor. In much the same way, inviting new and experienced teachers to participate in the disciplinary enterprise will certainly result in unforeseen conflicts and tensions—as well as possibilities. For instance, Amy Goodburn mentioned that when the TA portfolios were discussed with faculty from across the disciplines, one professor expressed "shock" that some of the student writing the portfolio author had profiled as "excellent" included grammatical errors. As Amy put it, "This moment raised for me one of the problems with 'making teaching visible' particularly when the reader's assumptions about standards for 'good writing' differ from the portfolio author's." Fortunately, Amy noted, the portfolio authors were not present at this meeting and did not have to take the brunt of the criticism (as she did).

But even if they had been present, it could be argued, this challenge would have introduced them to an issue that they will likely face once they are professors of English (and really, tensions they are already facing): competing conceptions of good writing; entitlement felt by instructors (in and) outside of English to impose their own criteria for good writing on the composition classroom; negotiations between one's own beliefs about good writing and writing instruction and pressures to "serve" other disciplines, and so on. While it might be safer to maintain the TAs' invisible status, it seems more productive to use a moment like this to help them consider—still from a relatively "safe" place—the political and rocky terrain that is occupied by first-year writing, and to help them imagine ways of teaching others about their work (while not closing down to others' ideas). Indeed, it is often the "messes" of our pedagogical work that require us to articulate our pedagogical goals, visions, and values—and to consider revision.

As the discipline of English studies has shifted (or claims to have shifted) its focus from the transmission of a canon to activities of engaging knowledge with others (Downing 1994)—a model that composition has always promoted—it is time, now, to prepare new professors of English to engage and teach a learning-centered discipline. It is time, too, to invite our colleagues from across disciplines to work with us on this revisionary work. While there will undoubtedly be conflicts, we might, as North argues, "harness the energy generated by the conflicts in order to forge some new disciplinary enterprise altogether" (2000, 73). By inviting new teachers to participate, from the start, in a learning-centered enterprise, we can not only help them negotiate the conflicts they will (and do) surely encounter as teachers and learners, but also work together to forge a new brand of disciplinary work—a brand that values teaching as intellectual lifework.

Notes

Introduction

1. A comprehensive description of this program is provided in Stephen M. North's (2000) *Refiguring the Ph.D. in English Studies*.

Chapter 1

1. I have found a few exceptions to this rule. For instance, the University of New Hampshire requires TA applicants to answer a series of teaching-related questions and to respond to a sample of student writing. The University of Arizona requires applicants to include a statement of teaching philosophy.

2. Composition scholars, however, have done well to make visible and challenge this disciplinary model. Most recently, Christine Farris and Chris Anson's collection *Under Construction: Working at the Intersections of Composition Theory, Research, and Practice* and Lynn Z. Bloom, Donald A. Daiker, and Edward M. White's *Composition in the Twenty-first Century: Crisis and Change*, have thoughtfully addressed these issues. Even so, as many contributors to these collections point out, composition has at the same time actively pursued traditional "disciplinary" status—a tendency I will touch on later in this chapter and will examine more fully in Chapter 2.

3. In 1963, Alfred H. Grommon edited *The Education of Teachers of English for American Schools and Colleges*, and Albert R. Kitzhaber authored *Themes, Theories, and Therapy: Teaching of Writing in College*. In 1965, John C. Gerber edited *The College Teaching of English*. Journals in English demonstrate a similar trend, as is evidenced by the abundance of articles on teacher training published between 1963 and 1967 in *College English* alone: Warner Rice's "The Preparation of College Teachers of English" (1963); Conrad Balliet's "On the Teaching of Literature" (1964); Jay Halio's "Teaching the Teaching Assistant"

(1964); John Jordan's "What We Are Doing to Train College Teachers of English" (1965); Don Cook's "Where Do Professors Learn to Teach? One Answer" (1965); Robert Carl Johnson's "Reflections on the Ph.D." (1965); and F. Parvin Sharpless's review of *The College Teaching of English* (1967). At no other time do this many articles appear on teacher training in a journal dedicated to the broad interests of English.

4. Of course, as I will suggest in the conclusion of this chapter, even as the programs were constrained, the graduates of these programs continue to engage in crucial pedagogical and scholarly work that promotes the pedagogy-centered vision of the D.A.

5. I have surveyed representations on department Web sites of TA training programs, course descriptions, and opportunities for ongoing development for those universities that offer Ph.D.s in rhetoric and composition. I am grateful to Susanne Stahl for her assistance in this research.

Chapter 2

1. Here I draw from Donna Qualley's (1997) notion of reflexivity, which she distinguishes from reflection. While self-reflection assumes individuals can reconsider past events independently of others, reflexivity "always occurs in response to a person's critical engagement with an 'other'" (11).

2. Maryellen Weimer notes, however, that most such journals do not demonstrate true cross-disciplinary conversations. Instead, they seem to function as their own "islands," rarely referring to one another (45).

3. The table of contents highlights the methodology employed—traditional research, classroom action research, or essay—in each article.

4. This does assume, however, not only that our methods of assessing scholarship can be transported to teaching, but also that they are necessarily effective. The Carnegie Foundation's 1992 International Survey of the Academic Profession, however, found that 45 percent of faculty felt that at their university "publications used for promotion decisions are just 'counted,' not qualitatively evaluated" (quoted in Glassick, Huber, and Maeroff 1997).

Chapter 3

1. On the other hand, we also see narratives where the teacher occupies the role of antihero. In confessing his or her pedagogical mistakes, and then providing a solution for "next time," he or she becomes even more of a hero.

2. I use "student" to refer specifically to moments when the writer was a student, and "learner" to refer to moments when the teacher is a "student" or learner in his or her own classroom.

3. All names have been changed.

4. An earlier version of this narrative was published as part of "Teacher Narratives as Interruptive: Toward Critical Colleagueship" (Gallagher, Gray, and Stenberg 2002).

Chapter 4

1. In Seitz's 2002 article "Changing the Program(s): English Department Curricula in the Contemporary Research University," he describes a plan in which graduate faculty are financially compensated for collaborating with others in different subfields to determine shared goals for their M.A. program's "core" courses.

Chapter 5

1. An important exception is the National Writing Project, where teachers from university and K–12 schools come together to meet as experts and to share best practices. However, as Gallagher notes, NWP is largely failing to attract newer members of the profession (2002, 189).

Works Cited

Adams, Charles. 2000. "The Real Small World(s)." *PMLA*. 115: 161–65.

Allen, Don Cameron. 1968. *The Ph.D. in English and American Literature*. New York: Holt, Rinehart and Winston.

Anson, Chris M., and Deanna P. Dannels. 2002. "The Medium and the Message: Developing Responsible Methods for Assessing Teacher Portfolios." In Minter and Goodburn, 89–100..

Arant, Darby. 2003a. Facilitation handout. Creighton University.

———. 2003b. Textbook review. Creighton University.

Balliet, Conrad A. 1964. "On the Teaching of Literature." *College English* 25, no. 8: 612–13.

Bartholomae, David. 1996. "What Is Composition and (if You Know What That Is) Why Do We Teach It?" In Bloom, Daiker, and White, 11–28.

Berlin, James A. 1987. *Rhetoric and Reality: Writing Instruction in American Colleges, 1900–1985*. Carbondale: Southern Illinois University Press.

———. 1996. *Rhetorics, Poetics, and Cultures: Refiguring College English Studies*. Urbana, IL: NCTE.

Bishop, Wendy. 1990. *Something Old, Something New: College Writing Teachers and Classroom Change*. Carbondale: Southern Illinois University Press.

Bloom, Lynn Z., Donald A. Daiker, and Edward M. White. 1996. *Composition in the Twenty-first Century: Crisis and Change*. Carbondale: Southern Illinois University Press.

Bolin, Bill, and Peter Vandenberg. 1995. "Introduction: A Forum on Doctoral Pedagogy." *Composition Studies*. 23, no. 2: 4–5.

Boquet, Elizabeth. 2002. *Noise from the Writing Center*. Logan: Utah State University Press.

Boyer, Ernest L. 1990. *Scholarship Reconsidered: Priorities of the Professoriate*. Princeton, NJ: Carnegie Foundation for the Advancement of Teaching.

Brannon, Lil. 1993. "M[other]: Lives on the Outside." *Written Communication* 10, no.3: 457–65.

Brannon, Lil, and Gordon Pradl. 1984. "The Socialization of Writing Teachers." In "Training Teachers, Part 2," special issue, *Journal of Basic Writing* 3:28–37.

Bridges, Charles W., ed. 1986. *Training the New Teacher of College Composition*. Urbana: NCTE.

Britzman, Deborah P. 1994. "Is There a Problem with Knowing Thyself? Toward a Poststructuralist View of Teacher Identity." In *Teachers Thinking, Teachers Knowing: Reflections on Literacy and Language Education*, edited by T. Shanahan, 53–74. Urbana, IL: NCRE and NCTE.

Brookfield, Stephen D. 1995. *Becoming a Critically Reflective Teacher*. San Francisco: Jossey-Bass.

Brunner, Diane DuBose. 1994. *Inquiry and Reflection: Framing Narrative Practice in Education*. Albany: SUNY Press.

Buck, Jo Ann, and MacGregor Frank. 2001. "Preparing Future Faculty: A Faculty-in-Training Pilot Program." *Teaching English in the Two-Year College* 28, no. 3: 241–50.

Carter, Kathy. 1993. "The Place of Story in the Study of Teaching and Teacher Education." *Educational Researcher* 22, no. 1: 5–12.

CCCC Task Force on the Preparation of Teachers of Writing. 1982. "Position Statement on the Preparation and Professional Development of Teachers of Writing." *College Composition and Communication* 33, no. 4: 446–49.

Chism, Nancy Van Note. 1998. "Preparing Graduate Students to Teach: Past, Present, and Future." In *The Professional Development of Graduate Teaching Assistants*, edited by Michele Marincovich, Jack Prostko, and Frederic Stout, 1–16. Boston: Anker.

Clandinin, D. Jean. 1992. "Narrative and Story in Teacher Education." In *Teachers and Teaching: From Classroom to Reflection*, edited Tom Russell and Hugh Munby, 124–37. London: Falmer.

Coles, William E., Jr. 1977. "Staffroom Interchange: Teaching the Teaching of Composition; Evolving a Style." *College Composition and Communication* 28, no. 3: 268–70.

Connors, Robert J. 1999. "Composition History and Disciplinarity." In *History, Reflection, and Narrative: The Professionalization of Composition, 1963–1983*, edited by Mary Rosner, Beth Boehm, and Debra Journet, 3–22. Stamford, CT: Ablex.

Cook, Don. 1965. "Where Do Professors Learn to Teach? One Answer." *College English* 27, no. 2: 114–18.

Cowan, Toni, Joyce Traver, and Thomas H. Riddle. 2001. "A TA Perspective of a Community College Faculty-in-Training Pilot Program." *Teaching English in the Two-Year College* 28, no. 3: 251–58.

Crowley, Sharon. 1998. *Composition in the University: Historical and Polemical Essays*. Pittsburgh: University of Pittsburgh Press.

Cushman, Ellen. 1998. *The Struggle and the Tools: Oral and Literate Strategies in an Inner City Community*. Albany: SUNY Press.

Daniell, Beth. 1994. "Theory, Theory Talk, and Composition." In *Writing Theory and Critical Theory*, edited by John Clifford and John Schilb, 127–40. New York: MLA.

Delandshere, Ginette, and Anthony R. Petrosky. 1994. "Capturing Teachers' Knowledge: Performance Assessment a) and Post-Structuralist Epistemology, b) from a Post-Structuralist Perspective, c) and Post-Structuralism, d) None of the Above." *Educational Researcher* 23, no. 5: 11–18.

Downing, David B. 1994. "Preface." In *Changing Classroom Practices: Resources for Literary and Cultural Studies*, edited by David B. Downing, xiii–xv. Urbana, IL: NCTE.

———. 2002. "Beyond Disciplinary English: Integrating Reading and Writing by Reforming Academic Labor." In Downing, Hurlbert, and Mathieu, 23–38.

Downing, David B., Patricia Harkin, and James J. Sosnoski. 1994. "Configurations of Lore: The Changing Relations of Theory, Research, and Pedagogy." In *Changing Classroom Practices*, edited by David B. Downing, 3–34. Urbana, IL: NCTE.

Downing, David B., Claude Mark Hurlbert, and Paula Mathieu. 2002. *Beyond English, Inc.: Curricular Reform in a Global Economy*. Portsmouth, NH: Boynton/Cook.

Works Cited

Drake University Dept. of English. 1992. "Curriculum Rationale."

———. Web site. http://www.drake.edu/artsci/english/home.html.

Eble, Kenneth. 1972. "Preparing College Teachers of English." *College English* 33, no. 4: 385–406.

Elbow, Peter. 1968. "The Definition of Teaching." *College English* 30, no. 3: 187–201.

Ellsworth, Elizabeth. 1988. "Why Doesn't This Feel Empowering? Working through the Repressive Myths of Critical Pedagogy." Paper presented at the Tenth Conference on Critical Theory and Classroom Practice, Dayton, OH, October 26–29.

———. 1989. "Why Doesn't This Feel Empowering? Working through the Repressive Myths of Critical Pedagogy." *Harvard Educational Review* 59, no. 3: 297–324.

Faigley, Lester. 1992. *Fragments of Rationality: Postmodernity and the Subject of Composition.* Pittsburgh: University of Pittsburgh Press.

Farris, Christine, and Chris Anson, eds. 1998. *Under Construction: Working at the Intersections of Composition Theory, Research, and Practice.* Logan: Utah State University Press.

Ferry, Christopher. 1998. "Theory, Research, Practice, Work." In Farris and Anson, 11–18.

Fish, Stanley. 1998. "Truth and Toilets: Pragmatism and the Practices of Life." In *The Revival of Pragmatism: New Essays on Social Thought, Law, and Culture,* edited by Morris Dickstein, 418–33. Durham, NC: Duke University Press.

Fleischer, Cathy. 2000. *Teachers Organizing for Change: Making Literacy Learning Everybody's Business.* Urbana, IL: NCTE.

Freire, Paulo. 1993. *Pedagogy of the Oppressed,* rev. ed. New York: Continuum.

Gallagher, Chris W. 2002. *Radical Departures: Composition and Progressive Pedagogy.* Urbana, IL: NCTE.

Gallagher, Chris W., and Amy Lee. *Writers at Work: Invitations.* New York: Pearson Longman, forthcoming.

Gallagher, Chris W., Peter M. Gray, and Shari Stenberg. 2002. "Teacher Narratives as Interruptive: Toward Critical Colleagueship." *Symplokē* 10, no. 1–2: 32–51.

Gebhardt, Richard. 1977. "Balancing Theory with Practice in the Training of Writing Teachers." *College Composition and Communication* 28, no. 2: 134–40.

———. 1997. "Preparing Yourself for Successful Personnel Review." In *Academic Advancement in Composition Studies*, edited by Richard C. Gebhardt and Barbara Genelle Smith Gebhardt, 117–27. Mahwah, NJ: Erlbaum.

Gerber, John C., ed. 1965. *The College Teaching of English*. New York: Appleton-Century-Crofts.

Giroux, Henry. 1988a. "Border Pedagogy in the Age of Postmodernism." *Journal of Education* 170, no.3: 162–81.

———. 1988b. *Schooling and the Struggle for Public Life: Critical Pedagogy in the Modern Age*. Minneapolis: University of Minnesota Press.

———. 1995. "Who Writes in a Cultural Studies Class? or, Where Is the Pedagogy?" In *Left Margins: Cultural Studies and Composition Pedagogy*, edited by Karen Fitts and Alan W. France, 3–16. Albany: SUNY Press.

Giroux, Henry A., and Peter McLaren. 1986. "Teacher Education and the Politics of Engagement: The Case for Democratic Schooling." *Harvard Educational Review* 56, no. 3: 213–38.

Glassick, Charles E., Mary Taylor Huber, and Gene I. Maeroff, eds. 1997. *Scholarship Assessed: Evaluation of the Professoriate*. San Francisco: Jossey-Bass.

Goodburn, Amy. 2002. "(Re)Viewing Teaching as Intellectual Work in English Studies: Insights from a Peer Review of Teaching Project." *Reader: Essays in Reader-Oriented Theory, Criticism, and Pedagogy* 47:83–108.

Gore, Jennifer. 1993. *The Struggle for Pedagogies: Critical and Feminist Discourses as Regimes of Truth*. New York: Routledge.

Graff, Gerald. 1987. *Professing Literature: An Institutional History*. Chicago: University of Chicago Press.

———. 1990. "Other Voices, Other Rooms: Organizing and Teaching the Humanities Conflict." *New Literary History* 21, no. 4: 817–39.

———. 1994. "The Pedagogical Turn." *Journal of the Midwest Modern Language Association* 27, no. 1: 65–69.

Works Cited

Grommon, Alfred H. 1963. *The Education of Teachers of English for American Schools and Colleges.* New York: Appleton-Century-Crofts.

Halio, Jay L. 1964. "Teaching the Teaching Assistant." *College English* 26, no. 3: 226–28.

Haring-Smith, Tori. 1985. "The Importance of Theory in the Training of Teaching Assistants." *ADE Bulletin,* no. 82: 33–39.

Harkin, Patricia. 1991. "The Postdisciplinary Politics of Lore." In *Contending with Words: Composition and Rhetoric in a Postmodern Age.* Ed. Patricia Harkin and John Schilb, 124–38. New York: MLA.

Hart, James Morgan. 1874. *German Universities: A Narrative of Personal Experience.* . . . New York: Putnam's. Quoted in Crowley 1998 , 55.

Haswell, Richard H. 1991. *Gaining Ground in College Writing: Tales of Development and Interpretation.* Dallas: Southern Methodist University Press.

Heath, Shirley Brice. 1983. *Ways with Words: Language, Life, and Work in Communities and Classrooms.* New York: Cambridge University Press.

Hjortshoj, Keith. 1995. "The Marginality of the Left-Hand Castes (A Parable for Writing Teachers)." *College Composition and Communication.* 46, no. 4: 491–505. Quoted in Seitz 1999, 17.

Holberg, Jennifer L., and Marcy Taylor. 2000. "Editors' Introduction." *Pedagogy* 1, no. 1: 1–5.

Hook, J. N., Paul H. Jacobs, and Raymond D. Crisp. 1970. *What Every English Teacher Should Know.* Urbana, IL: NCTE. Quoted in Gebhardt 1977, 35.

Huber, Mary Taylor. 2000. "Disciplinary Styles in the Scholarship of Teaching: Reflections on the Carnegie Academy for the Scholarship of Teaching and Learning." In *Improving Student Learning through the Disciplines: Proceedings of the 1999 Seventh International Symposium, Improving Student Learning,* edited by Chris Rust, 20–31. *Oxford: Oxford Centre for Staff and Learning Development.*

Hunt, Nancy. 2003. "Does Mid-Semester Feedback Make a Difference?" *Journal of Scholarship of Teaching and Learning* 3, no. 2: 13–20.

"Job Market Remains Competitive." 2000. *MLA Newsletter.* 6–7.

Johnson, Robert Carl. 1965. "Reflections on the Ph.D." *College English* 26, no. 4: 304–6.

Jordan, John E. 1965. "What We Are Doing to Train College Teachers of English." *College English* 27, no. 2: 109–13.

Kameen, Paul. 2000. *Writing/Teaching: Essays toward a Rhetoric of Pedagogy*. Pittsburgh: University of Pittsburgh Press.

Kitzhaber, Albert. 1963. *Themes, Theories, and Therapy: Teaching of Writing in College*. New York: McGraw-Hill.

Kleiner, Gail. 1999. "Getting to Know Each Other's Institutions." In *Looking Both Ways: High School and College Teachers Talk about Language and Learning*, edited by George Otte, 12–20. New York: CUNY Office of Academic Affairs. http://lbw.cuny.edu/pdf/book/intervisitation.pdf..

Knoblauch, C. H., and Lil Brannon. 1993. *Critical Teaching and the Idea of Literacy*. Portsmouth, NH: Boynton/Cook.

Krupa, Gene H. 1982. "Helping New Teachers of Writing: Book, Model, and Mirror." *College Composition and Communication* 33, no. 4: 442–45.

Kuklick, Bruce. 1990. "The Emergence of the Humanities." *South Atlantic Quarterly* 89, no. 1: 195–206. Quoted in Crowley 1998, 57.

Latterell, Catherine G. 1996. "The Politics of Teaching Assistant Education in Rhetoric and Composition Studies." Ph.D. diss., Michigan Technological University.

Lee, Amy. 2000. *Composing Critical Pedagogies: Teaching Writing as Revision*. Urbana, IL: NCTE.

Leverenz, Carrie Shively, and Amy Goodburn.1998. "Professionalizing TA Training: Commitment to Teaching or Rhetorical Response to Market Crisis?" *WPA* 22, no. 1–2: 9–32.

Lewis, Magda Gere. 1993. *Without a Word: Teaching beyond Women's Silence*. New York: Routledge.

Lord, Brian. 1994. "Teachers' Professional Development: Critical Colleagueship and the Role of Professional Communities." In *The Future of Education: Perspectives on National Standards in America*, edited by Nina Kressner Cobb, 175–204. New York: College Entrance Examination Board.

Lu, Min-Zhan. 1987. "From Silence to Words: Writing as Struggle." *College English* 49, no. 4: 437–48.

Luke, Carmen, and Jennifer Gore, eds. 1992. *Feminisms and Critical Pedagogy*. New York: Routledge.

Magner, Denise K. 1994. "Report to Focus on Standards for Assessing What Professors Do." *Chronicle of Higher Education*, 9 February, A22.

Malinowitz, Harriet. 1995. *Textual Orientations: Lesbian and Gay Students and the Making of Discourse Communities*. Portsmouth, NH: Boynton/Cook.

Marting, Janet. 1987. "A Retrospective on Training Teaching Assistants." *Writing Program Administrator* 11, no. 1–2: 35–45.

McLaren, Peter. 1988. "Schooling the Postmodern Body: Critical Pedagogy and the Politics of Enfleshment." *Journal of Education* 170, no. 3: 53–83.

McLean, S. Vianne. 1999. "Becoming a Teacher: The Person in the Process." *The Role of Self in Teacher Development*, edited by Richard P. Lipka and Thomas M. Brinthaupt, 55–91. Albany: SUNY Press.

McWilliam, Erica. 1994. *In Broken Images: Feminist Tales for a Different Teacher Education*. New York: Teachers College Press.

"Mellon Grant Awarded." 1999. *MLA Report to Members*. New York: MLA. 1.

Mettetal, Gwynn. 2001. "The What, Why, and How of Classroom Action Research." *Journal of Scholarship of Teaching and Learning* 2, no. 1: 6–13.

Miller, Susan. 1991. *Textual Carnivals: The Politics of Composition*. Carbondale: Southern Illinois University Press.

Minter, Deborah. 2002. "Peer Observation as Collaborative Classroom Inquiry." In Minter and Goodburn, 54–64.

Minter, Deborah, and Amy M. Goodburn, eds. 2002. *Composition, Pedagogy, and the Scholarship of Teaching*. Portsmouth, NH: Boynton/Cook.

MLA Committee on Professional Employment. 1998. "Final Report of the MLA Committee on Professional Employment." *ADE Bulletin* no. 119: 27–45.

Murphy, Michael. 2000. "New Faculty for a New University: Toward a Full-Time Teaching-Intensive Faculty Track in Composition." *College Composition and Communication* 52, no. 1: 14–42.

Murphy, Sean P. 2001. "Improving Two-Year College Teacher Preparation: Graduate Student Internships." *Teaching English in the Two-Year College* 28, no. 3: 259–64.

North, Stephen M. 1987. *The Making of Knowledge in Composition: Portrait of an Emerging Field.* Upper Montclair, NJ: Boynton/Cook.

———. 1996. "The Death of Paradigm Hope, the End of Paradigm Guilt, and the Future of (Research in) Composition" In Bloom, Daiker, and White, 194–207.

Stephen M. North, with Barbara A. Chepaitis, David Coogan, Lâle Davidson, Ron MacLean, Cindy L. Parrish, Jonathan Post, and Beth Weatherby. 2000. *Refiguring the Ph.D. in English Studies: Writing, Doctoral Education, and the Fusion-Based Curriculum.* Urbana, IL: NCTE.

Ohmann, Richard. 1976. *English in America: A Radical View of the Profession.* New York: Oxford University Press.

O'Neill, Peggy. 2002. "Constructed Confessions: Creating a Teaching Self in the Job Search Portfolio." In Minter and Goodburn, 33–42.

Orner, Mimi. 1992. "Interrupting the Calls for Student Voice in 'Liberatory' Education: A Feminist Poststructuralist Perspective." In Luke and Gore, 74–89.

Osborne, Randall E. 2000. "A Model for Student Success: Critical Thinking and 'At Risk' Students." *Journal of Scholarship of Teaching and Learning.* 1, no. 1: 41–47.

Otte, George. 2002. "High Schools as Crucibles of College Prep: What More Do We Need to Know?" *Journal of Basic Writing* 21, no. 2: 106–20.

Owens, Derek. 2001. *Composition and Sustainability: Teaching for a Threatened Generation.* Urbana, IL: NCTE.

Payne, Michelle. 1994. "Rend(er)ing Women's Authority in the Writing Classroom." In *Taking Stock: The Writing Process Movement in the '90s,* edited by Lad Tobin and Thomas Newkirk, 97–114. Portsmouth, NH: Boynton/Cook.

Phelps, Louise Wetherbee. 1991. "Practical Wisdom and the Geography of Knowledge in Composition." *College English* 53, no. 8: 863–85.

Qualley, Donna. 1997. *Turns of Thought: Teaching Composition as Reflexive Inquiry.* Portsmouth, NH: Boynton/Cook.

Ray, Ruth E. 1993. *The Practice of Theory: Teacher Research in Composition.* Urbana, IL: NCTE.

Rice, Warner. 1963. "The Preparation of College Teachers of English." *College English.* 24, no. 8: 635–38.

Ritchie, Joy S., and David E. Wilson. 2000. *Teacher Narrative as Critical Inquiry: Rewriting the Script.* New York: Teachers College Press.

Rose, Mike. 1989. *Lives on the Boundary: A Moving Account of the Struggles and Achievements of America's Educationally Underprepared.* New York: Penguin.

Ruddick, Jean. 1992. "Practitioner Research and Programs of Initial Teacher Education." In *Teachers and Teaching: From Classroom to Reflection,* edited by Tom Russell and Hugh Munby, 156–70. London: Falmer.

Scholes, Robert. 1998. *The Rise and Fall of English: Reconstructing English as a Discipline.* New Haven: Yale University Press.

Schroeder, Christopher, Helen Fox, and Patricia Bizzell. 2002. *Alt Dis: Alternative Discourses and the Academy.* Portsmouth, NH: Heinemann.

Seitz, James E. 1999. *Motives for Metaphor: Literacy, Curriculum Reform, and the Teaching of English.* Pittsburgh: University of Pittsburgh Press.

———. 2002. "Changing the Program(s): English Department Curricula in the Contemporary Research University." In Downing, Hurlbert, and Mathieu, 151–63.

Sharpless, F. Parvin. 1967. "Reflections on *The College Teaching of English.*" *College English* 29, no. 1: 32–39.

Shor, Ira. 1980. *Critical Teaching and Everyday Life.* Boston: South End.

Shulman, Lee S. N.d. "Course Anatomy: The Dissection and Analyses of Knowledge through Teaching." http://www.oswego.edu/multi-campus-nsf/course_anatomy.htm.

Slevin, James F. 1996. "Disciplining Students: Whom Should Composition Teach and What Should They Know?" In Bloom, Daiker, and White, 153–65.

Sosnoski, James J. 1994. *Token Professionals and Master Critics: A Critique of Orthodoxy in Literary Studies.* Albany: SUNY Press.

Stenberg, Shari, and Amy Lee. 2002. "Developing Pedagogies: Learning the Teaching of English." *College English* 64, no. 3: 326–47.

Stenhouse, Lawrence. 1985. "What Is a Curriculum?" In *Research as a Basis for Teaching: Readings from the Work of Lawrence Stenhouse*, edited by Jean Rudduck and David Hopkins, 67–69. Portsmouth, NH: Heinemann.

Sternglass, Marilyn S. 1997. *Time to Know Them: A Longitudinal Study of Writing and Learning at the College Level.* Mahwah, NJ: Erlbaum.

Swenson, Melinda M. 2001. "Preparing Teachers and Students for Narrative Learning." *Journal of Scholarship of Teaching and Learning* 1, no. 2: 1–14.

Tompkins, Jane. 1991. "Me and My Shadow." In *Feminisms: An Anthology of Literary Theory and Criticism*, edited by Robyn R. Warhol and Diane Price Herndl, 1079–92. New Brunswick, NJ: Rutgers University Press.

Tremmel, Robert. 1994. "Beyond Self-Criticism: Reflecting on Teacher Research and TA Education." *Composition Studies* 22, no. 1: 44–64.

Trimbur, John. 1996. "Writing Instruction and the Politics of Professionalization." In Bloom, Daiker, and White, 133–45.

Vandenberg, Peter. 1998. "Composing Composition Studies: Scholarly Publication and the Practice of Discipline." In Farris and Anson, 19–29.

Weimer, Maryellen. 1993. "The Disciplinary Journals on Pedagogy." *Change* November–December, 44–51.

Welch, Nancy. 1993. "Resisting the Faith: Conversion, Resistance, and the Training of Teachers." *College English* 55, no. 4: 387–401.

———. 1997. *Getting Restless: Rethinking Revision in Writing Instruction.* Portsmouth, NH: Boynton/Cook.

Worsham, Lynn. 1998. "Going Postal: Pedagogic Violence and the Schooling of Emotion." *Journal of Advanced Composition* 18, no. 2: 213–45.

Zeichner, Kenneth. 1983. "Alternative Paradigms of Teacher Education." *Journal of Teacher Education* 34, no. 3: 3–9.

INDEX

AUTHOR

Shari J. Stenberg is assistant professor and director of composition at Creighton University in Omaha, Nebraska, where she teaches courses in writing, composition theory, pedagogy, and literacy. She is also an active participant in the Nebraska Pre-K–16 Initiative, which brings teachers together across institutional boundaries to promote student and teacher learning. Her writing has appeared in *College English, Composition Studies, symplokē,* and the *Journal of Basic Writing.*

This book was typeset in Sabon by Electronic Imaging.
The typeface used on the cover was Stone Print Roman.
Cover calligraphy by Barbara Yale-Read.
The book was printed on 60-lb. Williamsburg Offset paper
by Versa Press, Inc.